# LEGAL RESEARCH GUIDE: PATTERNS AND PRACTICE

# LEGAL RESEARCH GUIDE: PATTERNS AND PRACTICE

## *Seventh Edition*

**Bonita K. Roberts**
*Professor of Law*
*St. Mary's University of San Antonio*
*School of Law*

**Linda L. Schlueter**
*Attorney at Law*
*Member, Texas Bar and District of Columbia Bar (Inactive)*

ISBN: 978-1-63281-534-7 (Print)
ISBN: 978-1-63281-535-4 (eBook)

**Library of Congress Cataloging-in-Publication Data**

Roberts, Bonita K., author
   Legal research guide : patterns and practice / Bonita K. Roberts, Professor of Law, St. Mary's University of San Antonio School of Law, Linda L. Schlueter, Attorney at Law, Member, Texas Bar and District of Columbia Bar (Inactive). --
Seventh edition.
      p. cm.
   Includes index.
   ISBN 978-1-63281-534-7 (softbound)
1. Legal research--United States. I. Schlueter, Linda L. II. Title.
   KF240.R63 2015
   340.072'073--dc23
2015022995

Carolina Academic Press, LLC
700 Kent Street
Durham, North Carolina 27701
Telephone (919) 489-7486
Fax (919) 493-5668
www.caplaw.com

Printed in the United States of America

# Acknowledgments

We want to express our thanks to the following individuals who provided the inspiration for this manuscript: Professor David A. Schlueter, for his constant encouragement and support of this project, and Professor Richard Wydick, for his inspiration to say it in simple English.

# *Preface*

The purpose of this book is to provide law students, attorneys, and others doing legal research a simple step-by-step guide to the basic hard copy research processes. The book is not designed as a textbook to give an in-depth explanation of the law and its sources. Rather, this guide should be used when the research processes are unfamiliar to the researcher either through inexperience or insecurity.

To underscore the common patterns in print form legal research, as well as to simplify comprehension of each research process, checklists appear throughout the text and are separately indexed to allow the reader instant access to particular procedures. Specific problems illustrate each process, enabling the reader to relate better to each step or to follow the process through by using the problem for actual research. Because legal issues are rarely so straightforward as to involve only one research process, some sample problems are used in more than one chapter to demonstrate the interrelationships between research procedures. An appendix provides additional practice problems, accompanied by a brief outline of the research sources.

Although the databases for computer assisted legal research have expanded dramatically since publication of the third edition, unlimited access to material online may not be affordable or available to all researchers. Consequently, many day-to-day research tasks are still more efficiently completed by traditional research methods. The focus of this book, therefore, remains the efficient use of the manual research processes. In this edition, however, there are sections on print, electronic, and Internet versions. The electronic version focuses primarily on Lexis Advance and WestlawNext. The Internet version is limited to Internet sites that we consider to be reliable and stable addresses that are not likely to change.

# *Table of Contents*

# Table of Contents

# Table of Contents

# Table of Contents

# Table of Contents

# Table of Contents

# Table of Contents

# Table of Contents

# Table of Research Checklists

# Chapter 1

# INTRODUCTION TO LEGAL RESEARCH

## A.  OVERVIEW

The practice of law involves many transactions, both oral and written, that depend upon legal research to provide appropriate support for each argument or position taken on behalf of clients. This is true, for example, whether that research appears in the form of a client letter, a memorandum to a supervising attorney, a brief to a court, or an oral argument. The process of identifying and finding relevant law is called legal research.

Traditionally, legal research has been done by "manual" research. In other words, the researcher had to go to the law library and find the law in print or "hardcopy" or in some form of microform such as microfilm and microfiche. Over the last 100 years, the publishers have made this process easier to access through better systems for accessing the law by subject matter instead of chronological order, providing detailed indices, and a system for updating the law.

But even with these advances, the researcher probably would not refer to the "good ol' days." With the advent of computers and the Internet, there also came changes in the way legal research could be done. Thus, there is now available legal information both in print form and in electronic databases. Each method of legal research has its advantages and disadvantages. To do legal research accurately, quickly, and efficiently, the researcher must have a basic understanding of each method. Each is an important component and is best suited to certain types of information.

The law and sources interpreting the law are voluminous. Each has its particular research tools and skills. At first, this may seem a little overwhelming. The good news, however, is that there is a pattern to the research which guides the researcher through the process and a practice which gives the researcher the confidence that if there is law on the subject that it can and has been found. It is the goal of this text to share that pattern and practice which will give the researcher the skill and knowledge of this important legal task of finding, analyzing, and communicating the law. The more the researcher utilizes these skills, the easier research becomes. Thus, the researcher is beginning on a journey that will be important in the practice of law.

## B.  UNDERSTANDING THE BASICS

Currently, legal information is published in three main formats — print or hardcopy, microform (such as microfilm and microfiche), and electronic. Traditionally, legal materials have been in print and microform formats. This text was designed to teach the analysis and patterns for manual legal research in these formats. Through the "electronic version" sections and this chapter, however, insights and resources will be shared on electronic research. It is not designed to teach the detailed mechanics of electronic research, as that is better taught through the hands-on training that is provided by LexisNexis (or Lexis) and Westlaw.

Even with the continuing and constant-growing electronic format, there are important reasons to understand how to research using print resources. These include:

1. Understanding the legal analysis of manual research in the print format helps the researcher because the organization and elements of electronic databases are based on the structure of printed material.

2. The researcher may not be able to find relevant sources in an electronic database. It is important to know the scope of the database. For example, the database may only contain cases back to a certain point. More significantly, there is a wide variety of treatises that are not available electronically. Furthermore, electronic tools probably do not contain an updating or verifying function unless the researcher is using Lexis Advance or West-lawNext.

3. Technology is always wonderful when it is working. There may be, however, times when the server is down or the researcher does not have access to a computer or the Internet.

4. Cost and time are usually concerns whether in a small law firm or a large one. Electronic research is more difficult when the researcher does not know the area of law as well, and therefore, it wastes both time and money. Although some research time may be passed on to the client as "billable hours," it may not be possible to do this for all or most of the time spent particularly if a large amount of time has been spent because the researcher could not efficiently find the information electronically.

At the beginning of any legal research project, certain things must be done. First, the researcher must identify the legally significant facts. Legally significant facts are those that will cause the outcome to turn in one direction or the other. This analytical process will be described in detail depending on whether the researcher is looking for a case, statute, or administrative materials.

Second, from the legally significant facts, the researcher must determine what the issue is. Determining the issue keeps the researcher focused instead of going down trails that are not relevant.

Third, there needs to be a determination as to whether manual or electronic research will be the most efficient tool for the researcher and cost-effective for the client.

Fourth, once the information is found, it must be updated to ensure that it is the most current law. The researcher has both an ethical duty and practical obligations to the client as well as being an "officer of the court." Needless to say, it would be, at a minimum, very embarrassing to discover from opposing counsel or the court that the information was no longer current. The court does not take kindly to such failings and there are consequences for that conduct which are discussed below.

Fifth, once the legal authorities have been found, the researcher must communicate the information. This can be in various forms including a letter to the client, memoranda to the supervising attorney, or brief to the court. The authorities must be properly cited in the document. This enables the reader to find and verify the law.

Although law school studies give the lawyer a good basic knowledge of the law, it is impossible for a lawyer to know all of the law. Therefore, it is important for the lawyer to know how to quickly, efficiently, and accurately find the law and update it for the most current information.

The ethical rules of our profession outline the role and obligations of an attorney. For example, it is an ethical requirement that the lawyer is competent and has provided the court with accurate information. The Preamble to the Model Rules states: "A lawyer, as a member of the legal profession, is a representative of clients, an officer of the legal system and a public citizen having special responsibility for the quality of justice." Canon 6 of the Code of Professional Responsibility states that lawyers are to know "these plain and elementary principles of law which are commonly known by well-informed attorneys, and to discover the additional rules which, although not commonly known, may readily be found by standard research techniques."

Failing to do competent legal research can not only be a costly mistake, but it can have serious consequences for both the lawyer and the client. Here are a few examples:

- In *Smith v. Lewis*, 530 P.2d 589 (Cal. 1975), *overruled on other grounds, In re Marriage of Brown*, 544 P.2d 561 (Cal. 1976), the court approved an award of $100,000 in a legal malpractice case against the defendant-lawyer who had failed to apply principles of law commonly known to well-informed attorneys and to discover principles readily accessible through standard research techniques. The court stated: "had defendant conducted minimal research into either hornbook or case law, he would have discovered with modest effort" that the state retirement benefits and federal benefits were at least arguably community property. *Id.* at 596. Furthermore, the court stated that "Even as to doubtful matters, an attorney is expected to perform sufficient research to enable him to make an informed and intelligent judgment on behalf of his client." *Id.*

- Incompetent research may also lead to attorney fees to the opposing party. In *Lieber v. ITT Hartford Ins. Center, Inc.*, 15 P.3d 1030 (Utah 2000), the court found the action was "clearly meritless." *Id.* at 1037. Hartford's brief asserted that the issue "is apparently one of first impression for this Court." In fact, however, it "was effectively decided by this court twenty years ago" in a prior case which Hartford did not even cite in its brief or use in argument. *Id.* To make matters worse, Hartford's statements clearly implied that the Connecticut Legislature endorsed the reasoning of the Connecticut Supreme Court and codified it in statute. The court stated, "That is not in fact what happened." *Id.* at 1038. Counsel needs to properly research the law and accurately state the law to the court.

- Counsel's carelessness in drafting and filing a complaint may lead to sanctions. *Rodgers v. Lincoln Towing Serv. Inc.*, 771 F.2d 194 (7th Cir. 1985). Rule 11 of the Federal Rule of Civil Procedure states: "The signature of an attorney or party constitutes a certificate by him that he has read the pleading, motion, or other paper; that to the best of his knowledge, information, and belief formed after reasonable inquiry it is well grounded in fact and is warranted by existing law or a good faith argument for the extension, modification, or reversal of existing law . . . . If a pleading, motion, or other paper is signed in violation of this rule, the court, upon motion or upon its own initiative, shall impose upon the person who signed it, a represented party, or both, an appropriate sanction, which may include an order to pay . . . a reasonable attorney's fee." Counsel's incompetence in handling the case by making "frivolous" and "worthless" claims "without first making a proper inquiry into the relevant law and facts" led to sanctions. *Id.* at 206.

- Counsel may receive a stern rebuke. *Massey v. Prince George's County*, 918 F. Supp. 905 (D. Md. 1996). The court cited the rules of professional conduct for "competent representation" and stated that it includes the ability to research the law. *Id.* at 908. In footnote 4, the court actually described how the Natural Language search method could be done on WestlawNext. The senior attorneys tried to argue that they had not been actively involved. However, the court rejected this argument stating that they are responsible if they signed their names to the brief or pleadings. *Id.*

- Counsel may face disciplinary action such as a suspension. *Attorney Grievance Comm'n v. Zdravkovich*, 762 A.2d 950 (Md. 2000). A lawyer was given an indefinite suspension for various violations of the rules of professional responsibility including filing an improper petition without consulting the federal statute. The court stated that "adequate preparation has long been recognized as part of a lawyer's responsibility to provide competent representation." *Id.* at 961. The disciplinary rules preclude a lawyer from handling a matter "without preparation adequate in the circumstances." *Id.* Furthermore, the failure to properly investigate the facts of a case prior to trial has led to discipline. *Id.* The comments to the rules state that "competent handling of a particular matter includes inquiry into and analysis of the factual and legal elements of the problem, and use of methods and procedures meeting the standards of competent practitioners. It also includes adequate preparation." Comment to MRPC 1.1. The court concluded that although the lawyer "possessed the ability to conduct such research, he inexplicably failed to do so." *Id.* at 962.

These examples demonstrate the importance of legal analysis, competent legal research, and adequate preparation. Thus, mastering the legal research skills necessary to analyze the facts, find and analyze the law, and represent a client are important aspects of law practice. This text will prepare you for your professional research and analysis obligations.

## C.  LEGAL SEARCH ENGINES

On the Internet, there is a massive amount of information. Thus, having a good search engine to get the researcher to the website that is most relevant is important. Each search engine searches its own database of websites for specific words and phrases and then provides the researcher with a list of web pages that contain those specific words and phrases. There are general search engines such as Google, but this would not be an efficient method of searching. Therefore, more specific law-related search engines have been developed.

The most relevant law related search engines include:

- Lawcrawler, along with Findlaw, is a search engine that helps the researcher access law-related information sites on the Internet through simple search terms and phrases. The researcher can not only search for cases and codes, but also for professionals, such as expert witnesses and investigators or lawyers in particular areas of practice.

- MegalLaw, along with LawBot, is a search engine that allows the researcher to search multiple search engines simultaneously. Many bar associations provide free access to Fastcase for legal research. Since 2013, Fastcase has added an authority check feature called "Bad Law Bot" which will indicate if a case has been reversed or overruled. To gain access to Fastcase, bar members simply login to their bar page.

- Google Scholar is a more specific search engine by Google that searches scholarly literature of various disciplines including law. The legal section has court decisions and law review articles. It provides full access to some articles and an abstract of books. It may not, however, be the most efficient search method.

## D.  COMMERCIAL OR FEE-BASED SOURCES

### [1]  Lexis Advance and WestlawNext

Lexis Advance and WestlawNext are the two main commercial services that have dominated the legal information electronic system. Lexis Advance is owned by Reed Elsevier and WestlawNext is now owned by Thomson Reuters. Both of these companies are large international corporations.

Both Lexis Advance and WestlawNext provide access to primary authority such as cases, statutes, and administrative materials as well as a variety of secondary authority, such as law review articles and treatises. These materials are located in databases which are constantly being expanded.

Access to Lexis Advance and WestlawNext has changed over the years. Both services now provide a Web format. The advantage to the Web format is that it provides greater flexibility to access Lexis Advance and WestlawNext. The researcher can access information in his or her office or on a mobile device such as a personal digital assistant (PDA). Having access wherever the attorney is located is a tremendous advantage. For example, if the court asks for legal authority for a proposition and the attorney only is given the lunch hour to find it, easy access to Lexis Advance and WestlawNext is a big advantage. But equally important is that the attorney knows how to effectively and efficiently use these electronic resources.

Before using either Lexis Advance or WestlawNext, the researcher should go through the analytical process of identifying the legally significant facts and key issues to be researched. Once this is done, the researcher should develop a search strategy to make the most efficient use of time. As a general rule, billing on the system begins as soon as the researcher logs on to Lexis Advance or WestlawNext. Pricing options vary. However, usually it is based on the time spent or the number of searches or both. Sometimes, a flat rate can be negotiated. In addition to general pricing, there may be extra charges for certain sources or special databases. Thus, the researcher must know the pricing plan for the particular law firm. This does not apply for academic or educational use for law schools who have unlimited access, but usage must be for academic or education purposes only. There may also be differences in what is offered for academic, solo practitioners, or large law firms which has an impact on the pricing.

Periodically, LexisNexis and Westlaw provide advancements in their systems. In 2010, Westlaw introduced WestlawNext which is the next generation of its online services. Likewise, LexisNexis introduced Lexis Advance for Solos to solo practitioners in 2010, and Lexis Advance for Law Schools and Lexis Advance for Associates in 2011. These new systems transform how users access and manage information.

Lexis Advance is built on a completely new and separate platform from LexisNexis at www.lexisnexis.com, with a new algorithm for searching and retrieving information. This new structure was based on thousands of interviews and evaluations by legal professionals. The goal was to make research easier and more efficient to conduct.

Lexis Advance provides comprehensive and enhanced case law and statutes from all state and federal courts; top secondary sources; a collection of jury verdicts, briefs, pleadings, and motions; expert witness transcripts, depositions, and curricula vitae and more. LexisNexis continually adds content. Lexis Advance offers an easy to use search interface that eliminates having to select a certain "library" or database before searching, with optional pre-search filtering for jurisdictions, content types or practice areas. These products also include new features for organizing, storing, and delivering research results, including Folders to save search queries, documents, and notes, and enhanced search History listings and sorting tools. With this new generation of online services, there is no need to select what type of search language to use before conducting a search; Lexis Advance automatically analyzes the query entered and determines whether it is best treated as a terms and connectors or natural language search. Basic "terms and connectors" searching is still available and pull-down options are available to help researchers construct this type of query.

WestlawNext was developed over five years after extensive research on how researchers were using Westlaw. Normally, the researcher would have to choose a database but this is no longer required, although possible to limit the search. The researcher also had to specify whether the search was Natural Language or Boolean style. Now, WestSearch runs the search as a more powerful Natural Language search unless it detects that terms and connectors are used thereby automatically recognizing the search format. It allows the researcher to instantly see what primary and secondary authorities are available as well as other documents, such as briefs and motions. Once the researcher sees what materials are available, a determination can be made as to whether the query was too narrow or too broad and modifications can be made. It also links to additional on-point content and ranks the document's importance. The search can be saved in folders which can be shared in shared folders.

WestlawNext uses a research pyramid. At the base of the pyramid is secondary authority such as state jurisprudence materials, its encyclopedia, *A.L.R.* series, and other treatises and law review articles which discuss the law but are not the law itself. These materials can give the researcher a discussion of the issue, and thereby be particularly helpful if this is a new area of the law or one that is unfamiliar to the researcher. These materials can also lead to other primary sources. In the next tier of the pyramid, primary authority consisting of cases, statutes, and administrative regulations are available. The researcher always wants to find and cite primary authority if it is available. At the final tier of the pyramid is updating the materials through a system that was developed by WestlawNext called KeyCite. Changes have also been made in this updating process to display the KeyCite information across the top of the page and to show the most negative citing reference on the same page as the case. Updating the material is a critical function in the research process as an attorney has a duty to find and cite accurate up-to-date information.

## [2]   Selected Other Fee-Based Sites

In addition to the two main commercial services of Lexis Advance and WestlawNext, there are other services available at potentially a lower cost. They are probably not as comprehensive or have the ability to update the information. In addition, they may specialize in particular legal information such as legal periodicals. Depending on what materials the researcher needs, they may be a cost effective option.

The following are a few selected options:

- Access on CD-ROM. In the late 1980s, publishers started making materials available on CD-ROM. These may include such materials as statutory and case law as well as treatises and form books. CD-ROMs had the advantages of saving space and costs and could be taken or used any place there was computer. The disadvantage is that even though the publisher usually provides updates on replacement disks at regular intervals, the information is only as current as the update. Therefore, the researcher will need to update the information using another source. Searching methods on a CD-ROM would be the same as searching on Lexis Advance or WestlawNext. Considering the current state of the technology, ability to quickly update, and reasonable pricing options, CD-ROMs are becoming obsolete.

- HeinOnline — www.heinonline.org — HeinOnline is a product of the William S. Hein & Co. It is a legal publisher, periodical subscription agent, and the world's largest distributor of legal periodicals. In addition to legal periodicals, its database libraries also contain state and federal materials, legal history materials, and foreign materials.

- Index to Legal Periodicals and Books (ILP) — www.hwwilson.com — is part of the H.W. Wilson Co. which was founded in 1898 and has provided print and now web services particularly for indexing legal periodicals. It indexes over 1,025 legal journals, law reviews, and bar association publications. It also has various other databases including "Legal Source" which focuses on legal topics such as criminal justice, organized crime, international law, and federal law.

- LegalTrac — www.gale.com — is available through the Gale Group. It corresponds to the Current Law Index which began in 1980 and indexes more than 900 key law journals, legal newspapers, and specialty publications from the United States, Canada, the United Kingdom, Ireland, Australia, and New Zealand.

- Loislaw — www.loislaw.com — is a commercial legal research service. It provides access to various databases including federal and state case and statutory law, constitutional law, and administrative law. The company has also included treatises, forms, and other practical materials from Wolters Kluwer companies of Aspen Publishers and CCH as well as its state bar partners and other sources. It is not as extensive as Lexis Advance and WestlawNext, but may be a little less expensive. Loislaw has a citator called GlobalCite, but it is not the same as *Shepard's* on Lexis Advance or KeyCite on WestlawNext. GlobalCite lists documents that cite the document in Loislaw's entire collection of databases.

- Versuslaw — www.versuslaw.com — is similar to Loislaw and a lower cost alternative to Lexis Advance and WestlawNext. Its emphasis is on opinions in the United States Supreme Court, Federal Circuit Courts, all State Appellate Courts, and selected tribal and foreign courts. Versuslaw has a citator called V.Cite, but it is not the same as *Shepard's* on Lexis Advance or KeyCite on WestlawNext. V.Cite produces a list of cases within the selected jurisdictions that have cited the case and the researcher can determine whether the subsequent cases have impacted the case in a negative way.

## E.  FREE WEBSITES

There are many law-related websites on the Internet that are free. Although they can be very helpful, there are several disadvantages. First, there are no laws or regulations that govern the accuracy of the content of a free website. Second, there is no requirement to update the information. Lawyers, on the other hand, have a duty to provide the court with both accurate and updated information. Third, from a research perspective, these sites usually do not contain the valuable research aids that are available in print or fee-based electronic research such as Lexis Advance or WestlawNext. Thus, the researcher must assess the best print or electronic source for the information.

## [1]  Selected General Websites

There are some reliable general websites that may be searched. Even though they are not comprehensive, they can provide a starting point. These include:

- www.abanet.org is the American Bar Association (ABA) site. The ABA is the leading national bar association for American lawyers. The website has information about the ABA, its publications, activities, and code of ethics. The ABA has a variety of sections that focus on specific areas of law such as Antitrust Law, Business Law, Family Law, International Law, Tort Trial and Insurance Practice. It also provides general information such as links to legal research sources, law school libraries, and branches of government. Briefs for cases before the United States Supreme Court are also available on the website.

- www.findlaw.com is one of the best and most comprehensive sites. It provides such information as case law, federal and state statutory law, directories for the government, law firms, and legal organizations, and law schools, and legal practice materials. The researcher can search by the type of authority, by jurisdiction, or by practice area. Thomson Reuters owns Findlaw. Although this is the parent company of WestlawNext, the content does not come from WestlawNext but through the text or PDF version of slip opinions. Sometimes there are links to WestlawNext and a credit card can be used as payment for the WestlawNext enhanced information.

- Hieros Gamos — www.hg.org — it was one of the first comprehensive online law and government information sites. It has over two million links and is international in scope. It also provides various lists such as for expert witnesses, forensic experts, investigators, and process servers.

- www.llrx.com is Law Library Resource Xchange and began in 1996. It provides such things as court rules, forms, and dockets, archived articles, European Union law, and other comparative and foreign law.

## [2]  Selected Federal Government Sources

Some of the main government sites include:

- www.usgovernmentmanual.gov. The Government Manual is the official handbook of the federal government. It includes information for the legislative, judicial, and executive branches of government. This publication will be discussed in later chapters.

- www.gpo.gov/fdsys/ is the Government Printing Office (GPO) website and provides online access to the Code of Federal Regulations, the Federal Register, the Congressional Record, and Congressional bills, documents, hearings, and reports. The system was upgraded to a digital system called FDsys which provides free online access to a long list of official Federal Government publications.

- www.loc.gov is the Library of Congress site and the researcher can find information and access to Congress and federal agencies. The Library of

Congress is the nation's oldest federal cultural institution and is the research library for Congress. It contains millions of books, recordings, photographs, maps and manuscripts in its collections. It also provides a large international studies of non-English materials as well as the law library that has foreign legislation.

- www.thomas.gov was started in 1995 to make federal legislative materials available to the public. It is maintained by the Library of Congress and provides legislative information such as the text of bills and resolutions, roll call votes by the House and Senate, committee reports, and public laws. However, the Library of Congress has a new platform which will replace Thomas sometime after 2014. It is Congress.gov and is currently operational.

- www.uscourts.gov is the home page for federal courts. It contains information for each of the federal courts and their rules and policies, judges, forms, fees, court records, and court statistics.

- www.USA.gov is the official web portal into various federal government online sources and websites. It links to either government owned, government sponsored, or quasi governmental agencies and websites such as the U.S. Postal Service.

- www.whitehouse.gov is the website for the President. It includes such documents as speeches and remarks, Executive Orders, Proclamations, and Presidential Memoranda.

## [3] Selected State and Local Sources

There are a variety of state and local sources. For example:

- State and local governments — www.statelocalgov.net — is a directory of official state and local government websites. It is organized by state and then what is available for statewide offices, the legislative, judicial, and executive branches of government, as well as for boards and commissions, regional entities, county entities, and city entities.

- www.municode.com is a website for local government documents such as municipal charters and ordinances. This is an important research tool because it has generally been difficult for the researcher to obtain a copy of these documents particularly if the researcher did not live in that particular city.

- State court websites provide a variety of information such as court rules, fees, forms, court preferences, and cases.

- State legislature websites provide various information including bills, statutes, state constitution, legislators, committees, hearings, calendars.

- State bar associations usually have sections for lawyers and the public. The bar association may provide access to free legal research.

## [4]  Selected Law School Websites

Today, most law schools have a website which provides a link to the school's law library. Some of the most comprehensive sites are:

- www.law.cornell.edu is Cornell Law School's Legal Information Institute (LII) which provides extensive legal materials such as constitutions, codes, court opinions, administrative materials, and foreign law.

- www.kentlaw.edu has a variety of sources online. It may be particularly helpful in historical research. Use the American State Papers for historical American law research. Find legislative and executive documents from 1789 through 1838.

- www.washlaw.edu is the website for Washburn University School of Law's legal resources on the web. It contains federal and state materials as well as foreign and international materials.

## F.  PROPER CITATION FORM

Once the legal authority is found, it must be properly cited. In your legal research course, you will learn how to cite various legal authority including cases, statutes, administrative regulations, legal periodicals, and legal books.

Citation form is important for several reasons. First, knowing how to cite the legal authority will save law students time and frustration in not having all of the information that is needed to properly cite the legal authority. Second, properly citing legal authority says something about the writer. Generally, if citation form is sloppy, the reader questions whether the research and legal analysis were also sloppy. Lawyers can quickly develop a reputation, good or bad, for their skill and abilities. Third, improperly citing the legal authority may mean that critical information was omitted that would help the reader find and verify the source. This is also a major problem. Fourth, "signals" are used at the beginning of the legal citation which tells the reader why the legal authority is being cited and how it supports the legal proposition. Signals need to be learned and used appropriately for a correct understanding of the legal proposition.

Traditionally, there has been one book that provided a uniform system of citation. It was called *"The Bluebook."* It began in 1926 by the law review editorial boards at Harvard, Yale, Columbia, and the University of Pennsylvania as a cost-saving measure, as typesetting footnotes at the time was expensive. It was called *The Bluebook* because of its blue cover. Over the years, *The Bluebook* has expanded in the number of pages and its explanation of legal citation. As the introduction to the 19th edition recognizes:

> For generations, law students, lawyers, scholars, judges, and other legal professionals have relied on *The Bluebook's* unique system of citation. In a diverse and rapidly changing legal profession, *The Bluebook* continues to provide a systematic method by which members of the profession communicate important information about the sources and authorities upon which they rely in their work.

Indeed *The Bluebook* became widely used and accepted as the standard for legal citation. However, it was not without its critics. Law students found it confusing and without explanation of the component parts to a citation. For the legal community, the Association of American Law Schools (AALS) complained of certain changes that were made in the 16th edition of *The Bluebook*. In particular, the AALS was concerned about the change in meaning of the introductory signals that told the reader why the authority was being cited and how it supported the legal proposition. At the 1997 annual meeting of the AALS, a resolution was passed and a formal request was made to reinstate the definitions of the signals. However, it was also resolved to provide an alternative to *The Bluebook* that would be written by legal educators.

In 2000, an alternative citation manual was produced and was called the *ALWD Citation Manual* (now known as *ALWD Guide to Legal Citation*). It was not intended to dramatically change the structure of citation form but to simplify the rules so that it would be easier to find, interpret, and apply them. *ALWD* also provides more examples on how to apply each rule.

*The Bluebook* remains the leader in legal citation form. Regardless of whether *The Bluebook* or *ALWD* is used, the principle of good citation form remains the same. It is well worth the law student's time to learn basic citation form.

---

## CHECKLIST FOR FORMULATING A SEARCH

1. Identify the legally significant facts.

2. Identify key words and phrases.

3. State the issue that needs to be researched as specifically as possible.

4. Determine the jurisdiction, *i.e.*, whether this is a general search or the researcher wants information in a specific jurisdiction.

5. Determine whether print or electronic research will be the most efficient tool for the researcher and cost effective for the client.

6. Formulate the query based on the terms that are most likely to be included in the type of resource that the researcher needs.

7. Check the date of the information and update the material as necessary.

8. Properly cite the legal authority.

# Chapter 2

# CASE LAW RESEARCH

## A. OVERVIEW

Everyone who enters law school becomes acquainted with the basic principles of law and legal logic in the substantive courses. The study of substantive law trains the student to recognize the legal issues confronted in practice on a day-to-day basis. An equally important task, however, is to locate the sources of that substantive law. The lawyer, then, needs to analyze carefully each legal problem first to determine what type of law is involved and then to find the law quickly and accurately. The importance of this legal research is underscored by the American Bar Association's Code of Professional Responsibility which requires understanding of both the principles of law and how to find them.[1]

Fortunately, legal research is a systematic process that lends itself to a step-by-step approach. The purpose of this guide is to explain and re-enforce these processes through the use of checklists which will help simplify the research process.

As mentioned in Chapter 1, doing legal research over the years has changed as there has been a greater move toward electronic research. This is particularly true in finding cases as some law libraries have discontinued print versions for materials that are available electronically.[2] But during the transition period, it is important for the researcher to be comfortable with both print and electronic copy as both are still being published and probably available.

---

[1] Canon 6 of the Code of Professional Responsibility states that lawyers are to know "these plain and elementary principles of law which are commonly known by well-informed attorneys, and to discover the additional rules which, although not commonly known, may readily be found by standard research techniques."

[2] American Bar Association (ABA) requires that a law school "shall keep its library abreast of contemporary technology and adopt it when appropriate." *See* Rule 601(c). It is also to maintain "core collection of essential materials" to support its students and facility. *See* Rule 606. But these are general requirements and will vary according to the particular library.

| THE PATTERN OF LEGAL AUTHORITY | | | |
|---|---|---|---|
| LEVELS OF AUTHORITY | *Federal* | *State* | *Local* |
| TYPES OF AUTHORITY | Constitution Statutes Cases Administrative Rules & Regs. | Constitution Statutes Cases Administrative Rules & Regs. | Municipal Charters Ordinances Administrative Rules & Regs. |

## [1]   Types of Authority

The American legal system is comprised of law from several levels of government and various types of authority. Legal authority is divided into two major categories: they are *primary* and *secondary* authority. These types of authority affect the research process because of their relative importance.

### [a]   Primary Authority

*Primary authority* is the law itself, and therefore, the most desirable source of legal research. Primary authority consists of written constitutions, statutes, and court decisions. These authorities are in turn designated as either *mandatory* or *persuasive*.

*Primary mandatory authority* consists of the constitution, statutes, and decisions of the highest level of courts from a jurisdiction. For example, all trial and intermediate appellate courts in California must follow the California constitution, statutes, and Supreme Court of California decisions. *Primary persuasive authority* consists of appellate court decisions from other jurisdictions. However, the constitutions or statutes from other jurisdictions are neither mandatory nor persuasive. Because primary authority is the most important source, the researcher should always try to locate primary authority to support the client's position.

### [b]   Secondary Authority

*Secondary authority* is all other written expressions of the law. As a rule, secondary authority explains or expounds upon primary authority. It is generally used if there is no primary authority to support or explain the legal issue. Examples of secondary authority include treatises, law review or bar journal articles, and legal encyclopedias.

| TYPES OF AUTHORITY | |
|---|---|
| PRIMARY: | State and Federal Constitution Statutes Cases — either mandatory or persuasive |
| SECONDARY: | State and Federal All other written expressions of the law |

The purpose of this chapter is to analyze *primary authority* in the form of cases, that is, judicial decisions, and to discuss the methods of finding that case law. The following chapters will discuss the other forms of primary and secondary authority.

## [2] The Foundation

The Anglo-American judicial system is founded on the concept of the "common law" and the doctrine of *stare decisis*. The term *common law* refers to the judicial decisions by English courts which were the basis of law for the states and countries originally settled and controlled by England. Thus, the term is distinguished from that body of law from other judicial systems such as Roman law, civil law, and canon law. Because American judicial decisions came from English common law, they are also referred to as the common law. The term, however, does not include statutes that are passed by the various federal and state legislatures.

From this concept of the common law, the doctrine of *stare decisis* emerged. Simply stated, the court will review the facts of "our case" to determine if they are the same or substantially similar to those in previous cases. These earlier cases are referred to as precedent. If the facts are similar, then the same law will be applied. If there are some differences or distinctions in the legally significant facts, then the court will not adhere to the principle of law announced in the precedent. Instead it will apply another rule or create a new rule, which in turn may become precedent for later cases. In some cases, even where the legally significant facts are identical, the court for policy reasons may not follow the precedent. This has the positive effect of adding flexibility to our law when the needs of society change.

The doctrine of *stare decisis* is fundamental to the American judicial system because of three inherent advantages. First, *stare decisis* promotes a sense of stability to our law. This is essential if there is to be public confidence in the judicial system. Second, *stare decisis* provides some predictability of the outcome of the case. It is important for lawyers to be able to advise their clients with confidence, and they can do so with a measure of certainty because of this doctrine. Third, *stare decisis* ensures fairness by the court. This means that individuals will be treated the same way given a certain set of facts. This doctrine is important to the legal researcher because it highlights the emphasis on *case law* to the American legal system. Therefore, every researcher's goal is to find a case "on point." This is the ultimate achievement in legal research!

## [3]  The Court System

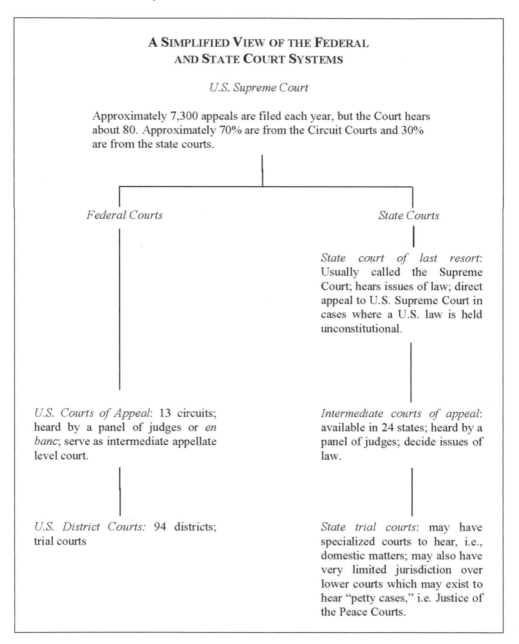

A SIMPLIFIED VIEW OF THE FEDERAL
AND STATE COURT SYSTEMS

*U.S. Supreme Court*

Approximately 7,300 appeals are filed each year, but the Court hears about 80. Approximately 70% are from the Circuit Courts and 30% are from the state courts.

*Federal Courts*

*State Courts*

*State court of last resort*: Usually called the Supreme Court; hears issues of law; direct appeal to U.S. Supreme Court in cases where a U.S. law is held unconstitutional.

*U.S. Courts of Appeal*: 13 circuits; heard by a panel of judges or *en banc*; serve as intermediate appellate level court.

*Intermediate courts of appeal*: available in 24 states; heard by a panel of judges; decide issues of law.

*U.S. District Courts:* 94 districts; trial courts

*State trial courts*: may have specialized courts to hear, i.e., domestic matters; may also have very limited jurisdiction over lower courts which may exist to hear "petty cases," i.e. Justice of the Peace Courts.

### *Structure and Reporting*

The courts on both the state and federal levels are organized in a similar structure, although the names of the courts may be different in each state. *Trial courts* hear testimony from witnesses or receive written documents as evidence. These courts decide matters of law and fact. As a general rule, trial court decisions are not reported. The exception to this rule is federal district court decisions; however, approximately 10–15% of these cases are reported.

If the trial court has committed prejudicial error, the case may be appealed to an *intermediate court of appeals*. These courts hear only issues of law and are bound by the facts that were introduced in the trial court. However, approximately 30–35% of the cases at the federal level are reported because all federal circuits have adopted rules restricting the number of published cases due to the heavy case load.

Some cases may be appealed to the *court of last resort* if there has been prejudicial error by the intermediate court of appeals. It should be emphasized that not all errors are grounds for appeal. The courts are not called upon to be perfect; they only need to be fair. In addition, the court of last resort is limited to questions of law that are presented in written briefs and in some instances oral arguments. All decisions from the court of last resort are reported, although in some instances, decisions involving disciplinary matters may be omitted.

### Unreported Decisions

If only a small percentage of cases are reported, then most cases are "unreported" or "unpublished." The courts have criteria as to whether a case will be published or not. For example, the Court of Appeals for the Fifth Circuit has Rule 47.5.1 which establishes the criteria for publishing a case. A legend on the first page of the opinion will indicate that the court has determined that this decision should not be reported.

Traditionally, unreported or unpublished cases had no precedential value. If the decision was made to not publish a case, then it was harder for lawyers to have access to the case, and as a practical matter, they were unavailable for citation. Thus, it would be unfair to allow citation to opinions that were not readily available to all lawyers. It also saved both judicial and litigant time and expense by not having read cases that may only be redundant of published cases which had precedential value.

The value of unreported cases has been a topic of discussion, debate, and controversy for years. In 2006, the United States Supreme Court adopted proposed Federal Rule of Appellate Procedure 32.1. Prior to its adoption, the proposed rule was hotly debated. The final version is considered a compromise. The rule became effective on December 1, 2006 and prohibits the federal courts of appeal from disallowing citation to federal unpublished opinions that are issued on or after January 1, 2007. Rule 32.1 also states that if an unreported case is cited, then the party must file and serve a copy of the opinion with the brief or other paper in which it is cited.

Although this brings uniformity as to whether they can be cited, each circuit still has discretion as to whether unreported cases will have precedential value. For example, the current local rules for the Fifth Circuit provide that unreported cases do not have precedential value except for cases concerning the doctrine of res judicata, collateral estoppel, or law of the case.[3] The local rules also provide that an unreported

---

[3] Local Rule 47.5.4.

decision may be cited if it has persuasive value concerning a material issue which has not been decided in a reported case.

However, the electronic era had an impact on bringing change of philosophy as to unreported cases as well as the accessibility of them. Lexis and Westlaw began making unreported cases available in their databases. In 2001, West began publishing the Federal Appendix®. It covers opinions and decisions from 2001 to date issued by the U.S. courts of appeals that are not selected for publication in the Federal Reporter. The format is similar to other West reporters with headnotes, key numbers, and synopses prepared by West's editors. Advance sheets ordinarily combine into one issue the Federal Reporter and West's Federal Appendix®. The researcher must carefully consider whether to use an unreported case in a memo or brief. Certainly, if there are reported cases on the same principle, the unreported case is merely redundant. It is essential that the researcher consult the local rules for each circuit to determine the use and applicability of an unreported case.

## B.   CASE LAW ORGANIZATION

Before examining the various methods of finding a particular case, it is important to review briefly the ways in which the cases are *reported*, *i.e.*, published.

### [1]   Official and Unofficial Reports

The decisions of the courts that are published are reported in *official* and/or *unofficial* reports. An official report is one that has been designated as such by the federal or state legislature. However, the terms "official" and "unofficial" do not indicate the quality or accuracy of a report. Both forms of publication include cases that have been designated by the court for publication and prepared by the clerk's office.

At the present time, 28 states have official reports. Some states have adopted "public domain" citations which allows for searching through traditional print versions as well as new technologies. Fourteen states have adopted a public domain citation and five states have both an official and a public domain citation. If there is an official report of the case, then it *must* be cited in that jurisdiction and it must precede any unofficial cite. For example, a traditional official cite is shown followed by the unofficial cite.

> *Barbee v. Queen's Medical Center*, 119 Haw. 136, 194 P.3d 1098 (Haw. App. 2008).

For states that have a public domain citation, it follows the same format but looks slightly different. It is cited by the case name, the year of the decision, the Postal Service's two letter state abbreviation, a page number, and a paragraph for the specific reference in the case. For example, Wyoming adopted a public domain citation format for cases decided after 2003.

> *Sullivan v. State*, 2011 WY 46 ¶ 1, 247 P.3d 879 (Wyo. 2011).

In addition, neither the term nor the order of citation reflect the importance or popularity of the reporter. The unofficial reports are by far more popular because they are published more quickly than the official reports and contain many research aids. In contrast, the official reports are very slow in being published and generally do not contain research aids.

## [2]  The Organization of Reported Cases

Court decisions may be published in three ways: by jurisdiction, by geographical location, or by subject matter.

### [a]  Jurisdiction

Using this type of organization, cases from a specific court or several courts within a system will be published together. For example, the United States Supreme Court decisions are published in the *United States Reports*. One would not find, for example, the decision of a California court in that publication. The *United States Reports* are the "official" version, but a collection of Supreme Court decisions may also be found in the *Supreme Court Reporter*, an "unofficial" reporter published by West Group, and *United States Supreme Court Reports* (L. Ed.), an "unofficial" reporter published by LexisNexis.

### [b]  Geography

Cases are also reported according to geographic areas. Several states in a regional area can be combined in a single reporter. For example, cases from Texas, Arkansas, Kentucky, Missouri, and Tennessee make up the *Southwestern Reporter*, another publication from Thomson Reuters.

### [c]  Subject Matter

Court decisions may also be reported according to subject matter. For example, Tax Court decisions (generally called "memos") and Bankruptcy Court opinions are reported in various loose-leaf services for those particular subjects.

## [3]  The Stages of Publication

To facilitate access to reported decisions, court reports are published in three stages.

### [a]  Slip Opinions

The quickest form of publication is the "slip opinion" which is issued on the same day as the court announces its opinion. The slip opinion, which is usually in typewritten form, simply reports the decision of a particular case and does not include the syllabus (summary of the case), index, or other research aids that are generally found in later editions. The United States Supreme Court is an example of a court that issues slip opinions. Slip opinions can be obtained from the clerk of the court or sometimes on a subscription basis.

## [b]  Advance Sheets

"Advance sheets" are the next quickest form of publication. These are paper bound pamphlets which contain a number of cases from a particular jurisdiction and are generally issued on a monthly basis. Several advance sheets in turn comprise one bound volume of a reporter. Advance sheets contain the same research aids, format, and pagination as the bound volume.

## [c]  Bound Volumes

After some delay, sometimes months or even years, the bound volumes are available. The typical features of a bound volume include: a table of cases, in which the cases are listed both in alphabetical order and according to state in the regional reporters; a table of the statutes that are construed by the cases; the opinions of the court; research aids; a subject index; an index of words and phrases that are defined in the cases; and court rules that are interpreted in the volume.

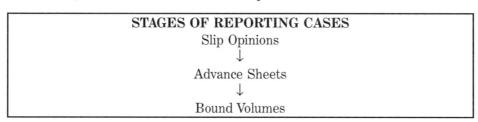

STAGES OF REPORTING CASES
Slip Opinions
↓
Advance Sheets
↓
Bound Volumes

## [4]  Subject Access

Because cases are published in chronological order in the bound volumes, researchers did not have *subject access* to the law. To remedy this problem, in 1897, John West, founder of West Publishing Company, devised a method for subject classification of legal and factual issues. He began by dividing the law into seven major *categories:* persons, property, contracts, torts, crimes, remedies, and government. These seven major categories were then subdivided into more than 400 legal *topics.* These topics were then divided into even more specific sections which were called *key numbers.* This subject arrangement of the law is collected in volumes called *digests.*

The *American Digest System* purports to list every reported state and federal case. It arranges cases according to topics and key numbers and states the principle of law in a short paragraph which is called an *abstract* of the case. Although West periodically adds new topics and key numbers as they are needed, it has maintained the original categories created by John West.

There are several types of digests. To find cases at both the state and federal levels, the *American Digest* should be consulted. Its volumes are divided according to years as follows:

|                     |                 |
|---------------------|-----------------|
| Century Digest      | 1658 to 1896    |
| First Decennial     | 1897 to 1906    |
| Second Decennial    | 1907 to 1916    |
| Third Decennial     | 1917 to 1926    |
| Fourth Decennial    | 1927 to 1936    |
| Fifth Decennial     | 1937 to 1946    |
| Sixth Decennial     | 1947 to 1956    |
| Seventh Decennial   | 1957 to 1966    |
| Eighth Decennial    | 1966 to 1976    |
| Ninth Decennial     | 1976 to 1986    |
| Tenth Decennial     | 1986 to 1996    |
| Eleventh Decennial  | 1996 to 2007    |
| Twelfth Decennial   | 2008 to current |

Due to the large volume of cases, the Decennials and General Digests are now in two parts. The Ninth Decennial was divided into two parts: Part I contains cases from 1976 to 1981 and Part II contains cases from 1981 to 1986. In addition, West introduced new topics and expanded old ones in the Ninth Decennial. Just as the Ninth Decennial was divided into two parts, the Tenth Decennial is also divided: Part I contains cases from 1986 to 1991 and Part II has cases from 1991 to 1996. The Eleventh Decennial Part 1 contains cases from 1996 to 2001, Part II from 2001 to 2004, and Part III from 2004–2007. The General Digest for the Twelfth Decennial began in 2008 to date. The disadvantage to the General Digest is that each topic has not been compiled into one volume. Therefore, the researcher must consult numerous volumes which is a very time consuming process.

The *General Digest* is the name for the current decennial before the 10-year period has occurred. For example, what will be the Twelfth Decennial is the current General Digest. It began in 2008 and will go for the next 10-year period.

In addition to the *American Digest System*, West publishes a *state digest* for every state except Delaware, Nevada, and Utah. In those states, the researcher must consult the corresponding regional digest. A state digest contains all state and federal cases reported within that state. In addition, there are "Library References" to *Corpus Juris Secundum (C.J.S.)*, West's legal encyclopedia, as well as "Research Notes" to a few other general publications.

*Regional digests* are also published for the regional reporters, with three exceptions. The Northeastern, Southern, and Southwestern regions currently do not have a digest. Access to the cases from these regions can be gained through the respective state digests.

Finally, there are digests for a single court or system of courts. The primary examples of these types of digests are the ones that publish federal cases. There is a series of digests for federal materials that include the *Federal Digest* (contains cases prior to 1939), the *Modern Federal Practice Digest* (1939 to 1961), *Federal Practice Digest* 2d (1962 to 1975), *Federal Practice Digest* 3d (November 1975 to 1989), and *Federal Practice Digest* 4th (1989 to present). Like the state digests, there are

"Library References" to *Corpus Juris Secundum (C.J.S.).*

There are several advantages to the digest system. First, the researcher is able to locate all cases on a particular point of law from the earliest time to the present. Second, research can be confined to a limited period of time, *i.e.*, a five to 10-year period. Third, the search can be as broad as the entire United States or as narrow as a particular state. Fourth, the digests list cases regardless of whether they cite each other or not.

However, there are some inherent disadvantages to the digest system. The researcher must keep in mind that these are only abstracts of the cases and not the opinions of the courts or even the holdings of the courts in all abstracts. Furthermore, the abstracts do not indicate whether the case has been overruled or is affected by a statute. Therefore, the *general caveats* in legal research apply to the digests: (a) the case itself *must* be read; (b) only the opinion should be quoted; and (c) all relevant cases *must* be "Shepardized" through Lexis or "KeyCite" through Westlaw. The digests are probably the most common means of finding a case, and they can be a valuable research tool when viewed with the proper perspective.

## C.  CASE LAW LOCATION METHODS

The purpose of this section is to demonstrate that legal research is an integrated process whereby numerous resources by various publishers can be used to find the information quickly. Because our legal system is based on the doctrine *of stare decisis*, it is important that the lawyer find a case that is factually similar. There are several methods by which a case can be located depending upon the information the researcher already has. The simplest methods will be described first.

### LOOKING FOR A CASE?

Do you have the case name? If so, use one of the following methods for the print version:

1. Plaintiff's Name: The Digest Table of Cases lists cases by the plaintiff's name. Using the plaintiff's last name, the researcher can also find the case on Lexis Advance and WestlawNext.

2. Defendant's Name: Some digests still have a separate Defendant-Plaintiff Table, but many have incorporated them into the Table of Cases. Using the defendant's last name, the researcher can also find the case on Lexis Advance and WestlawNext.

3. Popular Name: *Shepard's Acts and Cases by Popular Names* lists cases by their popular name. Using the popular name, the researcher can usually find the case on Lexis Advance and WestlawNext.

If you do not have the name of a case, use one of the following methods:

4. Definitional Method:

   a. *Words and Phrases* — "permanent edition" lists the definitions of words that have been defined by the court.

   b. *Words and Phrases* — "digest edition" — also lists the definitions of words that have been defined by the court.

   c. *Black's Law Dictionary* — defines words and phrases that have been defined by the court.

   d. Lexis Advance and WestlawNext can also provide definitions of words and phrases defined by the courts or legislature. There is also a dictionary function online.

5. Digest's Descriptive Word Index: Using key words and phrases in the appropriate Digest's Descriptive Word Index, the researcher can obtain information according to subject matter. Using Lexis Advance or WestlawNext, the researcher can use key words and phrases to find a case.

6. Digest's Topic Method: The Digest's Topic Method lists information according to West's topics and key numbers. The research can use the same approach on WestlawNext. Lexis has also developed a topic and key number system.

7. Secondary Source Method:

   a. *American Law Reports (A.L.R.)*: Analyzes cases on a narrow issue or topic. *A.L.R.* annotations are available both on Lexis Advance and WestlawNext.

   b. Treatises: They focus on a particular area of the law and can lead the researcher to cases or statutes on point. Some treatises are available on Lexis Advance or WestlawNext.

## [1]  Name Method

### [a]  Plaintiff's Name

#### [i]       Print Version

Assume that the researcher only has the name of a case and wants to find a copy of the decision. The simplest technique for finding a case is to go to the *Table of Cases* in a digest which lists all cases in alphabetical order by plaintiff's name. Here is an illustration:

> **EXAMPLE:** Assume that you want to find a federal case entitled *Abbey v. United States*. Employ the following steps:
>
> 1. *Bound Volume:* Go to the appropriate digest's *Table of Cases*. In this example, it is a federal case, and therefore, it would be in the *Federal Practice Digest*. If the digest has more than one series, as does the *Federal Practice Digest*, be sure to check the *Table of Cases* for the most recent series because it contains the cases for all series. In this example, the *Federal Practice Digest* is in the *Fifth Series*. The researcher would have to check the *Table of Cases* at the back of the cumulative pamphlet supplement entitled "Federal Practice Digest 4th and 5th." Check by alphabetical designation of the first name listed. The researcher would look under "A" for Abbey.
>
> 2. *Pocket Part:* If the case is NOT in the bound volume, check the pocket part located in the back of the bound volume. Some digests, like the *Federal Practice Digest*, have a *Cumulative Pamphlet* which supplements the main *Table of Cases* volumes instead of a pocket part so be sure to check it. As indicated, the *Abbey* case is in the cumulative pamphlet.
>
> 3. When you locate the case name you will also see the jurisdiction followed by the citation to the volume and page number where the case is reported. The *Abbey* case can be found in volume 745 of the *Federal Reporter*, Third Series, on page 1363. Following the citation is a list of topics and key numbers under which the case is classified in the *Descriptive Word Index*. The Descriptive Word Method will be explained later.
>
> 4. *Reporter:* Find the case in volume 745 of the *Federal Reporter, Third Series*, on page 1363. Read and update the case through *Shepard's* in print or on Lexis Advance or KeyCite with WestlawNext.

#### [ii]      Electronic Version

All United States Supreme Court cases are reported and available on Lexis Advance and WestlawNext. In addition some intermediate appellate decisions are submitted for publication according the court's rules and, therefore, available on Lexis Advance and WestlawNext. At the federal level, some trial level cases are reported. The using the plaintiff's name, the *Abbey* case can be found in the federal database.

## [iii]    **Internet Version**

There is also Internet access to cases, although there may be limitations depending on the database or court. At the federal level, United States Supreme Court cases from 1893 to present can be found through www.findlaw.com/casecode/supreme. Cases for the 13 federal Courts of Appeal can be found through www.uscourts.gov. At the present time, United States District Court opinions are available on the court's website. For example, cases for the United States District Court for the Northern District of Texas can be found on www.txnd.uscourts.gov.

There are fee based websites that provide information. PACER (Public Access to Court Electronic Records) provides summaries of cases searchable by case number or party name, but it requires registration and charges a fee. Another fee based service for federal appellate court cases is LOIS Law at http://Loislaw.com, but it is not as extensive or sophisticated as Lexis Advance or WestlawNext. State court decisions are also available. For example, Texas Supreme Court cases could be accessed through http://www.supreme.courts.state.tx.us. Texas Courts of Appeal are available through http://www.txcourts.gov/.

Recently, state bar associations are making Fastcase and Casemaker available to their members. Over half of the state bar associations provide this free service with bar membership. As of 2014, the Texas Bar is the first and only bar to offer both services free to its members.

With Fastcase, attorneys have access to cases from state and federal courts, constitutions, state statutes, annotated statutes from other states, administrative regulations, court rules, transactional access to newspaper articles, federal court filings, and legal forms. Through HeinOnline, which has the largest collection of law reviews in the world, attorneys can check these secondary sources. With its *Bad Law Bot* feature, cases that have been cited with negative history are flagged.

Casemaker is similar to Fastcase in that it provides both state and federal law, the Texas Administrative Code, Texas attorney general opinions, Texas case law since 1886, state constitutions, Texas session laws since 1995, state court rules, and Texas revised statutes. It has four other services to update the law. *Casecheck+* updates the law so that the attorney knows if the case is still good law. *CiteCheck* creates a table of the cases, checks the history of cited cases, and display any negative case history. *CasemakerDigest* is a feature where the attorney can receive daily summaries of state and federal appellate cases by practice area. *Subsequent History* determines writ and petition history of a case. *Statute Annotator* shows how the courts have cited, applied, interpreted, and construed each statute.

If you do not know where to search on the Internet, try a Meta-Index for cases and other primary and secondary authority. Cornell University provides one at www.law.cornell.edu, Georgia State University's index is at www.gsulaw.gsu.edu, and CataLaw at www.catalaw.com is a "catalog of catalogs of worldwide law" on the Internet.

## [b]   Defendant's Name

### [i]        Print Version

A case may also be found through the defendant's last name. The *Defendant-Plaintiff Table* is located in the earlier digest series. Each federal and state digest provides a list of cases in alphabetical order by the defendant's name. Note, however, that regional digests and the *American Digest* (except the Ninth and Tenth Decennials) *do not* contain a Defendant-Plaintiff table.

When given a case name to research, it is always a good idea to check the *Defendant-Plaintiff Table* if the case cannot be found in the *Table of Cases* to eliminate the possibility that the parties' names have been inadvertently reversed. However, West has changed its *Digest Table of Cases* by merging the *Defendant-Plaintiff Table* into the *Table of Cases* which makes it simpler and easier.

**EXAMPLE #1:** The researcher wants to find a Montana case that was decided around 1980 concerning the enforcement of a lessee's right of first refusal to the sale of a leased farm. All the researcher knows is that the defendant's name is Reely. Employ the following steps:

1. *Bound Volume:* This can be checked in the state, regional, or *American Digest.* If you are a lawyer in Montana or one who has access to the state digest, then you would go to the state digest. For our purposes, use the Ninth Decennial which covers cases from 1976–1981. In any of the relevant digests, go to the volumes where a case of that approximate date could be found. Look under "R" for Reely.

2. *Pocket Part:* Check the pocket part in the back of the bound volume of the state or regional digest if the case cannot be found in the bound volume. Once the case name is located, a citation to the reporter will be given.

3. *Reporter:* Since you have located the Montana case of *Tribble v. Reely* in the bound volume of the Defendant-Plaintiff Table, go to volume 557 of the *Pacific Reporter* at page 813 where the case begins. Be sure to read and Shepardize the case.

### [ii]        Electronic Version

The researcher can also find the defendant's name on Lexis Advance or WestlawNext using the same name search that was used to find the plaintiff's name. If the defendant's name appears in the database, the case will be retrieved.

### [iii]        Internet Version

As described above, cases can be found on the Internet. The researcher can find recent opinions on the court's official website. In addition, many states are providing Fastcase or Casemaker as a free benefit for bar membership.

## [c]   Popular Name

### [i]        Print Version

Another set of books that lists cases by name in alphabetical order is *Shepard's Acts and Cases by Popular Names*. This set is different from the *Table of Cases* in a digest because it does not include all cases. It contains only those cases, state and federal, that have a popular name. A popular name is descriptive of the case but does not usually include the parties' names.

EXAMPLE: Locate the "Black Watch Case." Employ the following steps:

1.  *Bound Volume:* Find the bound volume to *Shepard's Acts and Cases by Popular Names* and look in the last volume of the 1999 bound volumes under "Federal and State Cases" cited by popular name for the "Black Watch Case." Check under "B" for "Black Watch Case." The case is *Ingenito v. Bermec Corp.* You will find the abbreviation for the reporter where the case is located. In this example, it is volume 376 of the *Federal Supplement* beginning on page 1,154.

2.  *Supplementary Pamphlet:* If the case is not in the bound volume, check the supplementary pamphlet.

3.  *Reporter:* Find the case in volume 376 of the *Federal Supplement* at page 1,154.

### [ii]        Electronic Version

Specific terms such as "Black Watch" can be searched through Lexis Advance or WestlawNext. In the federal database, the researcher can use the term in the query. The same case, *Ingenito v. Bermec Corp.*, 376 F. Supp. 1154 (S.D.N.Y. 1974) will be found.

## [2]   Definitional Method

## [a]   Words and Phrases "Permanent Edition"

### [i]        Print Version

Whenever the researcher has a definitional problem, the first source to check are the volumes entitled *Words and Phrases*. These volumes appear in two forms. The first and most convenient form is the "permanent edition" of *Words and Phrases* which currently has 46 volumes in the series. These books help the researcher to locate cases, both state and federal, that have defined a word or phrase. The definitions are arranged in alphabetical order and use abstracts to state the court's definition of a word. In addition, if a word has several related terms, an index to these subordinate matters is listed and the abstracts are arranged according to the index format. This material is updated through annual cumulative pocket parts in the back of each volume.

The following problem illustrates the use of *Words and Phrases*.

**EXAMPLE:** Lisa Victim owns a home in Baton Rouge, Louisiana. During a hurricane, Victim's roof was damaged and had to be replaced. She called Reliable Roofing Company who employed Harry Worker. Around 3:00 p.m., Worker began descending a 30-foot ladder when he fell and suffered multiple fractures. An ambulance took him to the hospital where blood and urine tests showed he had a blood alcohol level of .160 and tested positive for cocaine. Based on this evidence, the worker's compensation insurer denied benefits. According to Louisiana law, did Worker meet the definition of "intoxication"? Use the following research steps:

1. The researcher should use the *Words and Phrases* volumes in either the *Louisiana Digest* or the *Words and Phrases* permanent edition.

2. *Bound Volume:* Locate the bound volume in the permanent edition for "intoxication." For this example, there are two Louisiana cases on point in the bound volume. One case is specifically on point, *Johnson v. Abraham Payton Roofing & Co.*, 761 So. 2d 30 (La. App. 4th Cir. 2000).

3. *Pocket Part:* In the *Words and Phrases* permanent edition, there is a 2006 new edition, and therefore, this case is in the bound volume. However, the researcher must always follow the proper updating procedures, such as checking the pocket parts, so that pertinent cases are not overlooked.

4. *Reporter:* Further updating should be done through the bound volumes and advance sheets of the *Southern Reporter* that have been printed since the last pocket part to *Words and Phrases* was published.

5. *Update:* Any relevant case, the *Johnson* case in this example, should be updated through *Shepard's* in print or on Lexis Advance or KeyCite on WestlawNext to ensure that it has not been overruled or modified.

Before a case can be cited as authority, the researcher must verify that it is still "good law," *i.e.*, that the case has not been reversed, overruled, modified, or excessively criticized. This final check is made by Shepardizing the case in the appropriate volumes of *Shepard's*. This final step in legal research is a *must*. On occasion, there are cases in the reporters where the court will reprimand counsel for not knowing that a case he has cited as authority has been overruled. This embarrassment can easily be avoided if the researcher remembers that the last step in legal research is to Shepardize all cases that are going to be cited as authority.

There are *Shepard's* volumes that correspond to each of the state and regional reporters. It is helpful to check both *Shepard's* volumes because each volume contains different information. For example, the state *Shepard's* contains references to *American Law Reports (A.L.R.)* annotations, law reviews, and Attorney General Opinions. Regional *Shepard's* contain cites to *A.L.R.* annotations and citations to cases in other jurisdictions that have cited this case. There may also be differences in the publication date. The regional *Shepard's* may be more current because of the differences in publishing the official and unofficial reports as discussed earlier.

To update a case, the researcher should follow these steps:

1. Find the appropriate set of *Shepard's* in the print version.

2.  Several books will be on the shelf so it is critically important to find the volume(s) that correspond to the reporter. Frequently, the first-year law student fails to check if the volume of *Shepard's* corresponds to the first or second series of the reporter. If the researcher is in the wrong volume of *Shepard's*, then the case has not been Shepardized.

3.  The listings are in numerical order by volume and then page number. Find the case by the appropriate numerical cite.

4.  Review the history of the case as well as the treatment of other cases. *Shepard's* indicates this by a small letter prior to the citation to the reporter. In the front of each *Shepard's* volume, there is a list of abbreviations. For example, "s" means it is the same case at a different level of proceeding, *i.e.*, trial level or appellate level; "r" means reversed; "a" means affirmed; and "d" means distinguished.

5.  The small raised letters after the reporter abbreviation correspond to the headnote number in the case. The researcher can save time by looking specifically to find the relevant headnote.

6.  Be sure to check all bound volumes and supplements to *Shepard's* where the case may appear. Each pamphlet *must* be checked or else the researcher has not Shepardized.

There are potentially a gold soft covered annual or semi-annual cumulative supplement and red soft-covered monthly supplements. On the cover of each of these volumes, there is a section entitled "What Your Library Should Contain" which lists the bound volumes and supplements that must be consulted. Each bound volume and soft cover supplement must be checked. For the most current information, go to Lexis Advance and Shepardize the case. Typically, new information is available within 24–48 hours from when *Shepard's* receives the information.

## [ii]    Electronic Version

*Shepard's* has been the means of updating case law, statutes, and other sources of law for over 100 years. It publishes nearly 200 different citators and has traditionally been available in print form. Effective July 1, 1999, Shepardizing is only available through Lexis Advance.

Since acquiring *Shepard's*, Lexis has made some improvements in the format and capabilities of *Shepard's* which make it easier and more productive for the researcher to use. One of the features of *Shepard's* was to provide headnote analysis for West's reporters. Recently, Lexis has developed headnotes which are being integrated into *Shepard's*. Researchers can restrict their *Shepard's* results by the Lexis headnote or Shepardize a Lexis headnote directly from a case.

For now, *Shepard's* is continuing to provide *Shepard's* analysis of West headnotes while developing the next generation of citation research and validation tools. West created its online citation service which is called KeyCite. Through a system of flags and stars, it warns the researcher of negative history and the depth of the court's treatment.

## [b]  Words and Phrases "Digest Edition"

### [i]      Print Version

The second type of *Words and Phrases* volume is the "digest edition." There are volumes entitled *Words and Phrases* at the end of each series of the state, federal, and specialized digests. These volumes contain the words that have been defined by the courts in that particular jurisdiction. The disadvantage to the digest editions is that the words only have citations to the cases in which they were defined, and not abstracts of definitions themselves. This information is updated through the annual cumulative pocket part at the back of each volume; the most recent information can be found in the *Table of Words and Phrases* in the bound volumes and advance sheets of the *National Reporter* system since the last printing of the annual pocket part.

### [ii]      Electronic Version

Like the *Words and Phrases* "permanent edition," relevant cases can be found and updated through either *Shepard's* on Lexis Advance or KeyCite on WestlawNext.

## [c]  Black's Law Dictionary

### [i]      Print Version

Dictionaries will be discussed in greater detail in the Secondary Source chapter. *Black's Law Dictionary* is in its 10th edition and has been completely updated. It contains more than 50,000 terms with twice as many sources quoted and cited as in the 9th edition. It will define a word or phrase and provide primary authority for support.

*Ballentine's Law Dictionary* contains over 40,000 definitions of legal terms "based on the actual construction of those terms by courts of last resort, with each case cited to the page on which the definition appears."

### [ii]      Electronic Version

*Black's Law Dictionary* is available on WestlawNext. *Ballentine's Law Dictionary* is available on Lexis Advance.

## [3]  Descriptive Word Method

### [a]  Print Version

There are three easy ways to find the appropriate topic and key number. The first is the Table of Cases Method (discussed above). Using this method, the researcher locates the appropriate headnote from a known relevant case. The headnote states the topic and key number and this information can then be used in the digest system. The Descriptive Word Method and the Topic Method will be discussed below.

```
┌─────────────────────────────────────────────────────────────────┐
│                  FINDING A TOPIC AND KEY NUMBER                   │
│   1.    Table of Cases Method                                     │
│   2.    Descriptive Word Method                                   │
│   3.    Topic Method                                              │
└─────────────────────────────────────────────────────────────────┘
```

The Descriptive Word Method is the most common starting point if the researcher simply has a fact situation with no leads from a relevant case or statute. The first step in finding a case is to analyze accurately and thoroughly your fact situation. Your analysis should center around five elements which are common to every case. These elements are:

1. *Parties:* These are persons of a particular class, occupation, or relationship. Examples of parties might be tenants, doctors, children, heirs, or any person who is necessary for the lawsuit to be resolved.

2. *Places and Things:* These are objects which are involved in the dispute or have caused the problem to exist, or places where the problem arose. These may include automobiles, sidewalks, public buildings, theatres, or amusement parks.

3. *Basis of the Action or Issue:* This category considers the wrong suffered by reason of another's neglect of duty, some affirmative wrong that was committed, some legal obligation that was ignored, or the violation of a statutory or constitutional provision. Examples include negligence, conversion of property, a violation of the child labor laws, or an illegal search and seizure.

4. *Defenses:* This category reviews the reasons in law or fact why the plaintiff should not recover. Acts of God, assumption of the risk, or infancy are some examples of defenses.

5. *Relief Sought:* This category analyzes the legal remedy that is sought by the plaintiff. For example, the plaintiff may seek punitive damages, annulment, or an injunction.

Each of these categories should be analyzed in detail. Try to think of as many different words as you can for each category. In selecting key words and phrases, think of synonyms, antonyms, or closely related words. If you are having difficulty thinking of different words, use a dictionary or thesaurus. It should also be noted that, depending on the problem, some categories will be more helpful than others. Examine a problem that illustrates this point:

**EXAMPLE:** The plaintiffs are California residents who are both males and want to obtain a California marriage license and marry each other in that State. On two occasions, they applied to the Clerk of Orange County for issuance of a marriage license but were denied because they are of the same gender. Other than their gender, they met the qualifications for a license. They are challenging the constitutionality of California's statutory prohibition on same-sex marriage and the federal Defense of Marriage Act (DOMA). Because of the state and federal issues, the suit was filed in federal court.

### Analysis

Using the recommended case analysis, the key words and phrases should be used to describe the parties, places and things, basis of the action or issue, defenses, and the relief sought. Some of the words and phrases that might be used are as follows:

1. *Parties:* homosexuals, same-gender, same-sex, Clerk of Orange County
2. *Places and Things:* California, Orange County, Clerk's Office, marriage license
3. *Basis of the Action or Issue:* marriage, meaning of marriage, Defense of Marriage Act (DOMA)
4. *Defenses:* standing to bring claim
5. *Relief Sought:* issuance of marriage license, declaratory and injunctive relief

As noted above, not all of the words in our analysis will be helpful nor will every category of words or phrases be helpful in a particular problem. Therefore, the researcher should begin with the most specific key words. If these words are too specific, then more general words can be used. For example, the categories of defenses and relief sought are not helpful in this problem because they are too general. The more specific terms of marriage and same-sex are the most helpful. Also be aware that the terms "homosexuals" and "same gender" are listed in the analysis because the researcher may not know how the publisher categorizes the entries. Therefore, think of the synonyms that could be used for "same sex."

### Descriptive Word Index

The researcher should go to the *Federal Practice Digest Descriptive Word Index.* The word "marriage" is a topic with a subheading of "same-sex." It refers the researcher to the topic of "marriage" and the key number 4.1. Under that key number, there are no helpful California cases. However, if the researcher checked the pocket part to the Index under marriage and same-sex, there is a reference to the topic "Marriage" and key number 17.5(1). This key number is helpful. Again, it emphasizes the need to always check a pocket part even in an index.

### The Appropriate Digest

The researcher should go to the bound volume of the *Federal Practice Digest* that contains the topic "Marriage." Most digests are now in several series such as the *Federal Practice Digest* which is in the Fourth Series and part of the Fifth Series. Because there is no Fifth Series volume of "marriage," at this time, the researcher should go to the Fourth Series. Under key number 17.5(1), there is the California case of *Smelt v. County of Orange,* 447 F.3d 673 (9th Cir. 2006). The researcher will also discover that an appeal was filed with the United States Supreme Court, however, certiorari was denied at 549 U.S. 959 in 2006.

The researcher should also review earlier digests. There may be an older relevant case in an earlier digest. Simply use the relevant topic and key number in the older digests and any pocket parts or supplementary pamphlets.

*Updating*

The pocket part and supplementary pamphlets of the digest's bound volume should be checked in the 2014 Cumulative Pamphlet for the Fourth and Fifth Series. There are no further entries for key number 4.1. There are, however, other cases for key number 17.5(1), but nothing for California. For updating for even more recent cases, the topic and key number can be used in the advance sheets of the *Federal Reporter* since the last volume covered in the pocket part or supplementary pamphlet. The last volume covered can be found in the front of the pocket part or supplementary pamphlet. The most recent information can be located through Westlaw as cases are usually available online within 24–48 hours.

In summary, law books are constantly being updated. Therefore, the researcher must ask: "How is this volume supplemented or updated?" The digests should be updated through annual pocket parts, supplementary pamphlets, if any, weekly advance sheets of the reporter, and ultimately, a new series. Once you have a topic and key number, the researcher can also obtain the most recent information through Westlaw.

By way of review, the following summarizes the research steps that are involved in this problem:

1.  Analyze the fact situation according to the parties, places and things, basis of the action, defenses, and relief sought to isolate key words or phrases.

2.  Use these key words in the Descriptive Word Index.

3.  The pocket part for the index must be checked for new entries.

4.  The specific volume of the digest must be checked for cases that are on point.

5.  If the researcher wants cases from other jurisdictions on the subject which would be primary persuasive authority, the topic and key number could be run through other state or regional digests or the American Digest System.

6.  The pocket part and any supplementary pamphlet of each digest should also be checked for the latest cases.

7.  For thorough research, the date of the pocket part should be noted so that the topic and key number can be run in the relevant General Digest volume and the advance sheets of the regional reporter.

8.  Read the relevant cases.

9.  Relevant cases must be updated in the proper volume of *Shepard's* in print or on Lexis Advance or KeyCite on WestlawNext to ensure that they have not been overruled or modified.

In summary, this exercise demonstrates several important research points. First, it is important to learn how to analyze your facts so that you can isolate key words and phrases which will lead you to similar cases. Under the doctrine of *stare decisis*, this becomes a critical factor as the researcher is looking for a similar case. Second, when a relevant topic and key number are located, they may be used in different digests. The researcher can go from a newer digest to an older one. Because most states have passed statutes similar to DOMA or have considered the same sex issue, it may be helpful to find primary persuasive authority in other states. The same principle is possible if we begin in a state digest and want to expand our research to a regional or national digest. Finally, it is imperative that the researcher update the information and Shepardize relevant cases.

## [b]   Electronic Version

Through a combination of key words and phrases, the researcher is able to do a subject-matter search for cases on Lexis Advance and WestlawNext. In addition to key words and phrases, the researcher can use "natural language" on both Lexis Advance and WestlawNext which simplifies the research query by phrasing the query as if describing the issue to another person.

A search may also be done by using terms and connectors. The search may be limited to one jurisdiction or expanded to a regional or national search. WestlawNext also provides access to West's digest system so that the researcher can do a search by topic and key number. Topics are given a number that corresponds to the alphabetical topics in the digests. The key number is preceded by the letter "k." For example, a researcher could find constitutional law cases on the freedom of speech and press by entering 92k90 in a relevant database. Cases since 1931 are available by using the topic and key number system on Westlaw. In addition, WestlawNext has developed "KeySearch" which utilizes the West Key Number System that identifies the terms and key numbers most relevant to the researcher's legal issue and creates the query.

Lexis-Nexis has also developed its own topic and headnotes. Like West, it offers topical access to cases. These headnotes are assigned by Lexis editors and are from the case language on a particular legal point. At this point, West has substantially more subjects with approximately 100,000 to Lexis 16,000. The researcher, however, can check both to determine if one system is better suited to the particular issue.

## [4] Topic Method

### [a] Print Version

Another method of finding a case in a digest is the Topic Method. As soon as the researcher becomes familiar with the topics that are used by West, it is possible to search for the most specific topic. Once that is found, the researcher can read the *"scope note"* which is provided by West to double check the analysis. The scope note indicates what material is covered within the topic. West also provides a *topic analysis* which is like a table of contents of the topic and key number subjects. From this analysis, the researcher can select the most appropriate key number.

We may use the same same-sex marriage problem to demonstrate that the same case can be found using the Topic Method. By searching the 435 topics, the researcher would discover that the topic "Marriage" was the most relevant topic. Turning to that section, the researcher would then review the scope note which states in part that it includes the marriage contract and its nature and creation.

Further inquiry of the topic would lead the researcher to the analysis section where the contents of the topic "Marriage" are outlined. Review of the contents would lead the researcher to the subtopic of "same-sex and other non-traditional unions" which is discussed at key number 17.5. This is the same topic and key number that was found through the Descriptive Word Method.

### [b] Electronic Version

Topics and key numbers are also available on WestlawNext. Lexis developed its own topics and key numbers which are available on Lexis Advance.

Review our discussion of the digests and locating relevant cases by a checklist of steps to remember.

## DIGEST CHECKLIST

Using either the print or electronic version, analyze the fact situation according to the parties, places and things, basis of the action, defenses, and relief sought in order to isolate key words or phrases.

**Print Version**

1. Locate the relevant topic and key number by:

    a. Using the plaintiff's name in the Table of Cases;

    b. Using the defendant's name in the Defendant-Plaintiff Table if there is one or the Table of Cases if they have been combined;

    c. Using key words and phrases in the Descriptive Word Index; or

    d. Analyzing the topics according to the Topic Method.

2. Use the relevant topic and key number through all the relevant state, regional, or federal digests.

3. Update the digest through:

    a. The pocket part;

    b. The supplementary pamphlet, if any;

    c. The appropriate volumes of the General Digest;

    d. The advance sheets of the regional reporter; and

    e. WestlawNext.

4. Read the relevant cases.

5. Update the relevant cases in *Shepard's* in print or Lexis Advance or KeyCite on WestlawNext.

**Electronic Version**

1. Locate the relevant topic and key number by:

    a. Using the name of the plaintiff;

    b. Using the name of the defendant;

    c. Using a descriptive word or phrase; or

    d. Using relevant topics.

2. Once a topic and key number are found through either the West or Lexis systems, it can be use in other state or federal databases.

3. Read the relevant cases.

4. Update the relevant cases in *Shepard's* on Lexis Advance or KeyCite on WestlawNext.

## [5]  *American Law Reports (A.L.R.)*

## [a]  Print Version

### [i]        Overview of *A.L.R.*

Cases can be found through the *American Law Reports.* The *American Law Reports (A.L.R.)* is a series of annotated reports that are currently published by Thomson-West. It has been called a "selective reporter" of appellate court decisions because the publisher's editors select and annotate cases that are relevant on a specific issue. It is not a reporter in the traditional sense. *A.L.R.* is one of the major research tools for finding case law. It is a secondary source for finding primary authority.

*A.L.R.* is published in six series and a federal series that includes *A.L.R. Fed.* (1969–2005) and *A.L.R. Fed. 2d* (2005 to present). In addition, the publisher developed a series of books called the *Total Client-Service Library.* This Library consists of an encyclopedia, form books, and other research and trial preparation aids. These books will be discussed in more detail in Chapter 8 concerning secondary authority. In *A.L.R.6th*, the "Total Client-Service Library" has been expanded and its name changed to "Research References." In 1996, Thomson acquired Lawyers Cooperative Publishing and further changes are being made.

Each series of *A.L.R.* was published during a limited time frame.

- *A.L.R.* (the first series) was published between 1919 to 1948 in 175 volumes. Most of these articles have been superseded by more recent annotations. Therefore, a researcher using this series must be sure to follow proper updating procedure.

- *A.L.R.2d* was published from 1948 to 1965 in 100 volumes. Again, the researcher must be sure to update any annotations found in this series due to the likelihood that it has been superseded or supplemented.

- *A.L.R.3d* was published in 1965 to 1980 in 100 volumes. For the first four years, *A.L.R.3d* contained both state and federal issues. However, in 1969, a new series was created, *A.L.R. Federal*, and now all federal materials are contained in this series.

- Beginning in 1980, *A.L.R.4th* was created and it contains only state topics. *A.L.R.4th* was published from 1980 to 1991 and has 90 volumes.

- The *A.L.R.5th* series was created in 1992 to 2005 and has 125 volumes.

- A new sixth series was created in 2005 and its format is similar to the fifth series. It was meant to succeed and not replace the fifth series and its format is similar. But it has expanded its research references to include a reclassified *A.L.R.* Digest with the key number system, references to WestlawNext's topical databases as well as news and business databases, references to relevant government or private websites, and references to appellate briefs and pleadings for the reported case. The illustrative case is now at the back of the volume.

Recently, *A.L.R.* started a new series to meet the demands of international practice. It is called *A.L.R. International*. There is an analysis of legal issues and case law from both English and non-English speaking countries such as Brazil, Russia, India, China, and Korea. The topics that are covered in this set are those arising under international conventions and treaties. Effective January 2010, *A.L.R. International* is also available online.

Over the years, the format of the annotations has evolved, but most of the following research aids will be found in *A.L.R.2d, 3d, 4th, 5th* and *6th*:

1. A *reported case*. This case precedes the annotation and illustrates the principles that are involved in the annotation. The case includes a summary of the decision, the procedural evolution of the case, headnotes (previously different from the ones by West), a highlight of the attorneys' briefs, and the court's decision. Beginning with the fifth series, the reported case is at the back of the volume.

2. At the beginning of the annotation is a box which refers the researcher to the relevant resources in the *Total Client-Service Library*. In *A.L.R.6th* series, it has been expanded and named "Research References."

3. The *scheme* or article outline of the annotation outlines what is covered and lists the major topics by their section number.

4. A *word index* helps the researcher quickly find relevant cases. As with the digest, it is helpful to have analyzed your fact situation and have in mind key words and phrases. The index contains both legal and common words such as things, acts, persons, and places.

5. The *Table of Jurisdictions* provides quick access to cases from a particular state. For example, if the researcher were searching for only Texas cases, the Table of Jurisdictions would quickly show whether there were any Texas cases in the annotation. If there were, it would list the particular section number within the annotation. In later volumes, the name was changed to the Table of Cases, Laws, and Rules. In the early volumes of *A.L.R. Federal*, this table was called the *Table of Courts and Circuits*. In later volumes, it was called Table of Cases. So if the researcher wanted to find only Fifth Circuit cases, the Table would give that information.

6. The *"Scope"* section of the text discusses the exact issue that is presented in a particular annotation. If a corollary point is "not included," then the researcher is referred to the proper annotation in one of the other series of books. In addition, information about previous or superseded annotations are noted.

7. The section entitled *"Related Matters"* cites other secondary authorities. These might include law review articles or treatises on the subject.

8. The *"Summary"* or *"Summary and Comment"* concisely states the law governing the annotated subject and provides relevant background materials.

9. The *"Practice Pointers"* section provides useful hints to the attorney in proceeding with the case. These insights are given for both parties and may include ideas for alternative theories of recovery or defenses.

10. Finally, the *text* of the annotation provides an in-depth and impartial analysis of the issue supported by relevant cases. It notes any applicable rules, the weight of the authority, and any trends. It should be emphasized that *A.L.R.* is only a case finder, and therefore, relevant cases must be read and Shepardized before they are cited.

## [ii]       Finding an *A.L.R.* Annotation

Finding an *A.L.R.* annotation is a relatively easy task. There are three methods of locating an annotation, depending upon the information the researcher already has.

---

### LOOKING FOR AN *A.L.R.* ANNOTATION?

Use one of the following methods:

1. *A.L.R. Index:* Analyze the fact situation according to the parties, places and things, basis of the action, defenses, and relief sought to isolate key words or phrases.

2. *A.L.R. Digest:* Use the same method described in method 1.

3. *Table of Laws and Regulations:* Use only for *A.L.R. Federal* when the title and section of a federal statute or federal rule and regulation is available and you want to locate an annotation on point.

4. *Electronic Version*: *A.L.R.* annotations can be found through Lexis Advance and WestlawNext in their *A.L.R.* databases.

---

### A.L.R. Index *Method*

The most common approach for locating an annotation is through the Index Method. Over the years the name of the index has changed as well as what each index covered. Finding an annotation index is now easier. In 1999, the *A.L.R. Index* was updated and revised. Furthermore, a single volume *Quick Index* began in 2000 and provides references to all annotations in *A.L.R.3d, 4th, 5th,* and *6th.* It will be replaced or supplemented periodically. The *A.L.R. Index* covered *A.L.R.2d, 3d, 4th, 5th,* and *Federal.* The *A.L.R. Quick Index* covered *3d, 4th, 5th,* and *6th.* For *A.L.R. Federal* and *A.L.R. Federal 2d,* there is a separate single volume *Quick Index* that will be replaced semi-annually.

In 2008, the *A.L.R. Index* was again revised. It now covers annotations for all series. This has simplified the research location method into one index. This is a significant improvement. It is important because the most commonly used method for finding an annotation is through the Descriptive Word Method in the *A.L.R. Index.* Key words and phrases can be used in the *Index* to find a relevant annotation.

**EXAMPLE:** Locate both an annotation concerning same sex marriage and *Smelt v. County of Orange,* the California case you found through the Descriptive Word Method, on the issue of same-sex marriage.

The researcher should use the recommended case analysis and select key words and phrases to describe the parties, places and things, basis of the action or issue, defenses, and relief sought. Again, the researcher should begin with the most specific key words in the *A.L.R. Index.* Marriage and same sex are the key words. If more specific words were not helpful, the researcher could use more general words.

Using the key word of "marriage," the researcher would find a subheading of "same-sex." Those words refer the researcher to an annotation concerning "marriage between persons of the same sex." The relevant annotation can be found at 1 A.L.R. Fed. 2d 1.

The researcher should go to that annotation. This volume was published in 2005, and therefore, the annotation would not cite the 2006 *Smelt* case in the bound volume. However, the researcher should check the pocket part. The pocket part added a new § 6.5 entitled "Abstention in federal constitutional challenge to same-sex marriage limitations." The *Smelt* case is cited in that new section.

### Digest Method

After acquiring Lawyers Cooperative, there was a total reclassification of the *A.L.R. Digest* to correlate to the West Key Number analysis. West's *A.L.R. Digest* replaces the *Permanent A.L.R. Digest* for *A.L.R., First Series, A.L.R.2d Digest* for *A.L.R.2d,* and *A.L.R. Digest* for *A.L.R.3d, 4th, 5th,* and *Federal.* Like West's digest system, there are over 400 major topics that are further subdivided into more specific information. Thus, the researcher has available topics and key numbers. In addition, the Digest leads the researcher to *Am. Jur.* (American Jurisprudence) products, *C.J.S.,* and other specialized and practice-oriented publications within Thomson-West publication family.

### Table of Statutes, Regulations, and Rules Method

Issues involving federal materials such as statutes, regulations, and rules may be found through this method. The Table, which is located in the last volume of the *A.L.R. Fed. Tables* volumes, would show where the Federal Rules of Civil Procedure, Federal Rules of Criminal Procedure, Federal Appellate Procedure, Federal Rules of Bankruptcy, the rules of the United States Supreme Court, and Rules of United States Claims Court are cited in the annotations.

## [iii]     Updating an Annotation

Once an annotation has been found, it must be updated. Over the years, the publisher has developed an update method which has become easier with more recent series.

In *A.L.R.* (First Series), it was a cumbersome system of using a separate set called the *A.L.R. Blue Book of Supplemental Decisions.* Thus the researcher had to go to a separate set of books to update the annotation and any supplement pamphlets as well as checking the Annotation History Table. Similarly in *A.L.R.2d*, the series utilized a separate set called the *Later Case Service*. The researcher had to check the *Later Case Service* bound volume and its pocket parts as well as Annotation History Table. With all other series, the researcher could check the pocket part to the bound volume and the Annotation History Table.

If a topic of law is substantially changed, then *A.L.R.* will indicate that it has been "superseded" which means it has been replaced. Usually an annotation simply needs to be supplemented with new material and not completely replaced. *A.L.R.* will indicate that it has been supplemented. In either case, the researcher must review the new annotation.

To update an annotation, the researcher should:

1. *Read and Analyze the Annotation:* Once an annotation has been found, read the text and check the research aids such as the Scope of the Annotation, Related Matters, Practical Pointers, and Table of Jurisdictions. The cases that are cited in the annotation are listed on the Table of Jurisdictions. This helps the researcher to quickly find a case in the relevant jurisdiction.

2. Check the pocket part at the back of the bound volume.

3. *Annotation History Table:* Check the History Table in the *A.L.R. Index* by volume and page number of the annotation to determine whether it has been supplemented or superseded. For example, the annotation at *1 A.L.R. Fed. 2d* has not been superseded. The History Table in the pocket part should also be checked.

4. *Shepard's* Citations for Annotations is available for *A.L.R. 3d, 4th, 5th, 6th,* and *A.L.R. Federal.* Update through *Shepard's* in print or on Lexis Advance or KeyCite on WestlawNext.

5. *Latest Case Service Hotline:* West is now providing this hotline through a toll-free number that provides an attorney with the cites to relevant cases since the last supplement.

## [iv]    Updating the Case Law

Updating the case law is another important step in the process to find more recent case law relevant to the annotation. Check the chart at the end of this chapter for the specific details of each series. The researcher should note that the update process is different for *A.L.R.* and *A.L.R.2d* as described above.

1. *Bound Volume:* Using the example above, locate the bound volume for 1 A.L.R. Fed. 2d 1. Each annotation has an index with more specific words. Key words and phrases can be used to find the most relevant section of the annotation. Go to that section.

2. *Pocket Part:* Check the annual pocket part by following the section number from the bound volume. Normally, the researcher follows the same section number from the bound volume to the pocket part.

However, in this example, there is a "Table of New and Retitled Sections." In this new § 6.5 the California case of *Smelt v. County of Orange* can be found.

3.  *Reporter:* Once the case law is located, read the decision in the relevant reporter. In this example it would be the *Federal Reporter*.

4.  *Update:* All relevant cases must be Shepardized in the appropriate *Shepard's* set in print or on Lexis Advance or KeyCite on WestlawNext.

## [b]   Electronic Version

*A.L.R.* annotations are available through Lexis Advance or WestlawNext. There are several ways that a reference to *A.L.R.* can be found by using Lexis Advance. First, through key words and phrases that may appear in the title, a specific annotation may be found. If a full-text search were done, the words may lead to other unrelated issues. Second, Lexis Advance will automatically retrieve annotations meeting the search specifications in the GENFED library with "Federal Cases and A.L.R. Combined" or in the STATE library with "State Cases and A.L.R. Combined." However, Lexis Advance usually has an extra charge for seeing the annotation. Finally, if the researcher finds a case and uses the Auto-Cite command, all annotations citing the case are listed.

WestlawNext has also added *A.L.R.* as a database and it is updated every two weeks. An Annotation can be found by using either Natural Language or Terms and Connectors. Starting with the 5th series, *A.L.R.* added an "Electronic Search Query" in its "Research Sources" at the beginning of the annotation to aid the researcher in finding additional cases. Sample queries are done for Lexis Advance and WestlawNext. In 1992, Lawyers Cooperative (now Thomson Reuters) published an interim pamphlet which provided this information for each annotation in the 4th series.

| Series | Dates | Find | Update |
|---|---|---|---|
| *A.L.R.* **SUMMARY** | | | |
| First | 1919–1948 | *Quick Index; A.L.R. Digest;* Table of Cases | *Blue Book of Supplemental Decisions* and its Supplement Pamphlet; Annotation History Table |
| Second | 1948–1965 | *A.L.R. Index; A.L.R. Digest* | Later Case Service and its Pocket Part; Annotation History Table |
| Third | 1965–1980 | *A.L.R. Index; A.L.R. Digest* | Pocket Part; Annotation History Table, *Shepard's* Citations for Annotations, and Lexis or Westlaw |
| Fourth | 1980–1991 | *A.L.R. Index; A.L.R. Digest* | Pocket Part; Annotation History Table, *Shepard's* Citations for Annotations, and Lexis or Westlaw |
| Fifth | 1992–2005 | *A.L.R. Index; A.L.R. Digest* | Pocket Part; Annotation History Table, *Shepard's* Citations for Annotations, and Lexis or Westlaw |
| Sixth | 2005–Present | *A.L.R. Index; A.L.R. Digest* | Pocket Part, Annotation History Table, *Shepard's* Citations for Annotations, and Lexis or Westlaw |
| Federal | 1969–2005 | *A.L.R. Quick Index;* Table of Statutes, Regulations, and Rules; *A.L.R. Digest* | Pocket Part; Annotation History Table, *Shepard's* Citations for Annotations, and Lexis or Westlaw |
| Federal 2d | 2005–Present | *A.L.R. Quick Index;* Table of Statutes, Regulations, and Rules, *A.L.R. Digest* | Pocket Part, Annotation History Table, *Shepard's* Citations for Annotations, and Lexis or Westlaw |

---

### *A.L.R.* CHECKLIST

1. Analyze the fact situation to find key words and phrases.

2. Find a relevant annotation by using:

   a. The *A.L.R. Index*;

   b. The *A.L.R. Digest* Method for all series; or

   c. The Table of Statutes, Regulations and Rules in *A.L.R. Federal.*

   d. Through Lexis Advance or WestlawNext.

3. Read all of the annotation or the relevant sections.

4. Update the annotation by:

   a. The *Blue Book of Supplemental Decisions* for *A.L.R.* (first series), any supplement pamphlets, and Annotation History Table;

   b. The *Later Case Service* for *A.L.R.2d* and its pocket part and the Annotation History Table; and

   c. The pocket part and Annotation History Table for *A.L.R.3d, 4th, 5th, 6th,* and *Federal.*

   d. Update through *Shepard's Citations for Annotations* if using the print version. On the electronic versions of Lexis Advance or WestlawNext, the *A.L.R.* databases are made current by the weekly addition of relevant new cases as they are available from the publisher. On WestlawNext, for example, KeyCite history will indicate whether the *A.L.R.* annotation has been superseded by subsequent annotations.

5. Read all relevant cases.

6. Update all relevant cases through *Shepard's* in print or on Lexis Advance or KeyCite on WestlawNext.

---

## D. CITATIONS TO LEGAL SOURCES

Once the legal authority is found, the researcher must present that authority in legal memoranda to the senior partner or brief to the court. Statements that are made in a memo or brief must be supported by some type of authority. Arguments are not won on a lawyer's opinion — it is based on the facts and source of authority. As discussed earlier in this chapter, there is a hierarchy of authority. Thus, primary authority has greater weight than secondary authority. Primary mandatory authority has greater weight than primary persuasive authority. There is even a hierarchy of secondary legal authority as will be discussed in Chapter 9 of this text.

The reference to the source of the information or principle is called a citation. Citations are required in office legal memoranda, court briefs, and scholarly writings such as law review articles. Accuracy is critical because if the location of the information is incorrect, the reader will not be able to find the information at that location. Legal citation form is important because it tells the reader how to find the information and who is responsible for the information.

For example, in the case that was found in the same-sex marriage problem, *Smelt v. County of Orange*, 447 F.3d 673 (9th Cir. 2006), that citation gives the reader certain information on who the parties are, where the case can be located, who authored the opinion, and date that it was decided. In reviewing each part of the citation, the researcher specifically knows the following:

- The parties are Smelt and the County of Orange;
- The case can be located in volume 447 of the *Federal Reporter, Third Series* at page 673;
- The author of the opinion is the Court of Appeals for the Ninth Circuit; and
- The date that the opinion was decided is 2006.

It is important to master citation form for several reasons. First, it saves the researcher time. Instead of having an incomplete cite and thereby having to go back to the library to get the information, the researcher knows what information is needed and provides the correct cite initially. Second, it makes memos and briefs look more polished and professional. Using proper citation form gives an air of competence and professionalism. Third, it provides a better reputation and respect by senior partners, other lawyers in the profession, and the courts. Sloppy citation form raises the question as to whether the research and reasoning is thorough and accurate. An immediate impression is given by simply looking at the citation form in a memo or brief. A good reputation is important and the lawyer should always try to put his or her "best foot forward."

For almost 100 years, *The Bluebook: A Uniform System of Citation* (*Bluebook*) has provided a standard for citation form. It has been the main citation guide since 1926 when it was first published by the Harvard Law Review Association. It presents a different set of rules for memos and briefs, and with each edition, there were slight changes in the rules. Unfortunately, it has not been easy to use, particularly for students. In earlier editions, there was no explanation as to what a citation is or its component parts.

Due to the criticism of the *Bluebook*, the Association of Legal Writing Directors created the *ALWD Citation Manual: A Professional System of Citation* (now called *ALWD Guide to Legal Citation*) (*ALWD*) in 2000. It was designed to be easier to understand and to use by providing for a single set of rules for all forms of legal writing. *ALWD* tried to unify and simplify the teaching and use of citations. It has gained in popularity and is now adopted in over 90 law schools as well as many law reviews and courts.

Whichever system of citation form is adopted, it is important to be accurate and consistent. A good reputation is hard to establish, but a bad reputation can be gained immediately. Good citation is one way to demonstrate the researcher's competence and professionalism. Take a few minutes to learn basic citation form for primary and secondary authority.

## E.  ADDITIONAL TIPS

When preparing for a trial, there are additional things that practitioners would want to know. This section in each chapter will discuss helpful information that saves the practitioner time. The caveat is that the practitioner must always make sure the information is appropriate for his/her client and does not contain language that would be detrimental to the case.

As more materials become available online, there are a variety of places where it may be found. Our focus will be on Lexis Advance, WestlawNext, and some of the more popular sources.

1.  Finding a judge's profile and how he/she has ruled on a particular type of case. It is important to know something about the judge that the practitioner will appear before. For example, in WestlawNext Profiler it gives the contact information for the judge, the position held on the court, educational background, admitted to practice, certifications and specialties, honors, past legal positions held, and affiliations. The Profiler can also provide reports concerning experts challenged for admissibility; litigation history report includes such things as the judge's caseload, types of cases, parties, clients, and law firms; and the judicial reversal report analyzes the judge's trial and appellate history.

2.  Finding verdicts in similar type cases in a particular jurisdiction. Verdicts and settlements are available online and can be tailored to various amounts, jurisdictions, judge, law firm, and docket number. For example, MoreLaw.com provides a free database for jury verdicts and settlements. Lexis Advance also provides a Verdict & Settlement Analyzer Service.

3.  Finding an expert witnesses. Many cases will need an expert witness. WestlawNext has expert witnesses who have testified, their resume, as well as their deposition, declarations, affidavits, or trial transcripts. The practitioner can find an expert in a particular area who could provide expert testimony at trial. Hieros Gamos at http://www.hg.org/experts/expertises.html has a variety of litigation support including expert witnesses, forensic experts, investigators, and process servers.

4.  Finding jury instructions. The state and federal courts have patterned jury instructions on their sites. They can also be found through Lexis Advance and WestlawNext.

5.  Finding pleadings and motions. Various forms are available on Lexis Advance and WestlawNext. For example, LexisNexis Communities Portal at http://linkon.in/yORjKu. It has over 6,000 free forms from the extensive Matthew Bender® collection. These are continuously updated

and organized by topic and jurisdiction. There is also a Pay Forms section the practitioner can pay for a particular form if a free form is not available. In addition, federal agency forms can be found at USA.gov. At http://www.usa.gov/Topics/Reference-Shelf/forms.shtml there are federal forms and applications by agency name.

6. Finding voir dire questions. Practitioners ask jurors questions either orally or through questionnaires. Winning cases begins from the very beginning of the trial, and therefore, asking the right questions and properly assessing the jury is very important. WestlawNext has sample questions. For example, it provides two questions concerning punitive damages in personal injury cases which explain the purposes of punitive damages and how the juror feels about awarding them. It also asks if the juror is opposed or not opposed to such an award. Preparing and educating the jury of the evidence to come later in the trial is an important first step.

7. Finding briefs. Briefs are available on both Lexis Advance and West-lawNext. They can provide a wealth of information on legal issues and primary and secondary authority. PACER (Public Access to Court Electronic Records) provides summaries of cases searchable by case number or party name, but it requires registration and charges a low cost fee. It includes complaints, answers, and some briefs that were filed in federal district and appellate court cases and bankruptcy cases. The American Bar Association (ABA) provides briefs on the merits and amicus briefs filed at the United States Supreme Court for free at http://www.americanbar.org/publications/preview_home/alphabetical. html. There is also a calendar of cases to be heard.

8. Finding docket information. When a case is filed, the court assigns a number which is called a docket number. Each court maintains its own docket. On both Lexis Advance and WestlawNext, the researcher can find the case if the docket number is known.

9. Finding public records. Practitioners need to know information about clients, businesses, or potential witnesses. LexisNexis public records uncover hidden connections even when there is not a record in common. This can help the practitioner spot important issues from conflicts of interest to criminal records. The collection has more than 37 billion records from diverse sources such as public, private, regulated, and derived data.

10. Finding court rules. Practitioners must be familiar with the court rules. The rules address all aspects of court procedure such as word limits, filing instructions, and service of process requirements. Failure to follow the rules can have serious consequences. The easiest way to find the court rules is to go on the court's website. For example, the website for the United States Court of Appeals for the Fifth Circuit is http://www.ca5. uscourts.gov/ and its home page has a link to "Federal and 5th Circuit Rules of Appellate Procedure." As demonstrated in the example in this

chapter on unreported cases, it is important to know the local rules of a particular court.

11.   Finding ethical rules. Practitioners need to know the ethical rules of the profession. These rules provide the standards for the profession. For example, there are conflict of interest rules which govern whether a practitioner can accept a client, confidentiality rules as to information which must be kept confidential between an attorney and his/her client, and competence rules as to legal knowledge, skill, thoroughness and preparation reasonably necessary to represent clients. The ABA Center for Professional Responsibility makes these rules and interpretive comments accessible online at http://www.abanet.org/cpr/.

# Chapter 3

# UNITED STATES CONSTITUTIONAL LAW RESEARCH

## A. OVERVIEW OF THE LEGISLATIVE SYSTEM

Legislative materials are the second form of primary authority. As discussed in Chapter 2, the main goal of the researcher is to find primary authority to support the client's position. The constitutions and statutes on both the federal and state level constitute such authority.

Federal legislative material is based on the hierarchy of law. This law consists of three tiers. Article 6 of the United States Constitution declares that the Constitution is the supreme law of the land. Thus, the Constitution becomes the first tier of legislative materials. However, the United States Constitution also enumerates certain powers to Congress in Article 1, Section 8. Using these enumerated powers, Congress passes statutes. This type of legislation forms the second tier. Congress also has the authority to create administrative agencies to make the day-to-day rules and regulations that implement the statutes. These agencies' rules and regulations become the third tier.

| HIERARCHY OF AUTHORITY |
| :---: |
| Constitution |
| ↓ |
| Statutes |
| ↓ |
| Administrative Rules and Regulations |

In addition to the legislative enactments, the Constitution implicitly provides a check and balance system that includes the judicial branch of government. This means that the United States Supreme Court and the other created courts have the power to interpret the constitutional, statutory, and administrative rulings.

All of this law has a tremendous impact on legal research. To do a thorough job of legal research, the researcher must find the law on all three tiers as well as any judicial opinions that interpret each of these laws. Due to the volume of material, the beginner may become overwhelmed and conclude that this must be the most difficult form of legal research. However, once the research process becomes more familiar, the researcher begins to understand that researching legislative materials is a relatively straightforward procedure.

Because the United States Constitution is the supreme law of the land, our discussion will begin at this point.

## B.   CONSTITUTIONAL LAW LOCATION METHODS

The initial question that may perplex the researcher is why a constitutional provision is needed. It is apparent that one would try to find such a provision if the client's problem raised a direct constitutional issue. However, a less obvious reason is that the researcher may need to find the authority for a statute or administrative rule or regulation. Whenever there is a question of legislative or administrative authority, the researcher should consider the possibility that the authority is based on a constitutional provision.

There are many treatises, law review articles, and other secondary sources that provide a wealth of information about the historical background of the Constitution and its provisions. The researcher simply needs to be aware that such resources are readily available through the card catalog of any library. However, the text of this section will focus on the other research tools for finding the appropriate constitutional provision and interpretive case law.

The text of the United States Constitution may be found in the codes for federal statutory materials. For example, it may be found in the official publication, the *United States Code (U.S.C.)*. However, the major emphasis of this chapter will be placed on the two unofficial annotated codes, the *United States Code Annotated (U.S.C.A.)* (published by Thomson-West) and the *United States Code Service (U.S.C.S.)* (published by LexisNexis), because they are the publications that the researcher most frequently uses due to the research aids that are available and the annotation of judicial opinions.

All three of these codes are organized in the same manner. The constitutional provisions are listed in order of article and section number or amendment numbers. The statutory volumes are arranged according to subject matter and statutes are placed in 50 subject titles. However, the research procedure for finding a provision is the same for all of the codes. Because there are no references to interpretive cases in the *U.S.C.*, the unofficial annotated codes are more commonly used.

There are several important differences between the two unofficial codes because of the different philosophies between West and LexisNexis. West purports to provide comprehensive coverage of all federal and state cases. Also, West will refer the researcher to its publications such as the digests, encyclopedias, practice books, and form books. In contrast, LexisNexis provides fewer cases but longer abstracts and will refer the researcher to the Total Client Service Library which contains mostly secondary authority.

---

### LOOKING FOR A U.S. CONSTITUTIONAL PROVISION?

Does the subject matter raise a constitutional issue; is there a statute that implements the Constitution; or is the authority of the administrative agency questioned? If so, use one of the following methods:

1. Descriptive Word Method: Use the key words and phrases in the General Index of the constitutional volumes.

2. Topic Method: Go to the volume on that subject and then use the specific Individual Subject Index. *Note:* There are no cross references in the codes which lead the researcher to the constitutional provision.

Do you have a case that interprets a constitutional provision and you want more cases on this point? If so, use one of the following methods:

3. Look under the Index of Notes of Decision in the *U.S.C.A.* or *U.S.C.S.* for the constitutional provision you are researching and find the most appropriate note. Then check the bound volumes, pocket parts, and pamphlet supplements, if any.

4. Obtain the topic and key number from the "one good case" and use it in the various federal digests.

---

The following example will demonstrate how a constitutional problem can be researched when a direct constitutional issue is involved.

**EXAMPLE #1:** The defendant was arrested at the Orlando International Airport for the possession of cocaine. After he had checked his baggage, a suspicious Drug Enforcement Agent had Zeke, a trained canine, examine one of the bags. Zeke immediately detected the presence of contraband. Having been convicted in the federal district court, the Defendant raises a constitutional error on appeal. The issue before the court of appeals is whether the use of dogs trained in drug detection constitutes a "search" under the United States Constitution.

## [1]  Topic Method

If the researcher has some familiarity with constitutional law, it is apparent that this is a search problem which is controlled by the Fourth Amendment. Thus, by using the Topic Method, the researcher would simply find the volumes in the *U.S.C.A.* or the *U.S.C.S.* that deal with the Fourth Amendment.

## [2]  Descriptive Word Method

The Descriptive Word Method is the most common starting point if the researcher simply has a fact situation but does not know what constitutional provision will provide the answer. This method requires a more thorough analysis of the problem. To analyze this issue, the researcher should use the TAPP rule which is commonly used for statutory analysis. TAPP is an acrostic for Things, Acts, Persons, and Places.

Some of the words that might be used in our illustration are:

| | |
|---|---|
| Things: | search, trained dogs, luggage, baggage, rights, restrictions |
| Acts: | possession of cocaine, drugs, contraband |
| Persons: | Drug Enforcement Agency agent, traveler |
| Places: | airport |

## C. FINDING AND UPDATING A CONSTITUTIONAL PROVISION

### [1] Print Version

1. *Index Bound Volume:* Use the key words and phrases in one of the two indices. The first is the Constitutional Index which is at the end of the last constitutional volume. Under the phrase "searches and seizures," there is a reference to the Fourth Amendment. However, the Constitutional Index is a small index, and therefore, if the researcher has any difficulty in locating the provision, the four-volume current General Index at the end of the statutory law code volumes can be consulted. Many words are listed under the term "searches and seizures" in that volume. Adding the subdivision "rights" or "restrictions," however, would also refer the researcher to the Fourth Amendment.

2. *Index Pocket Part:* Index information as well as all other materials must be updated in the pocket part of the bound volume. Thus, the pocket part to the Index for the Constitution must be checked. However, there are no new entries. If the researcher uses the General Index, there is no pocket part because it is published annually in a softbound cover. This softbound format has been used since the mid-1980's.

3. *Read and Analyze the Provision in the Bound Volume:* The researcher must read carefully the constitutional provision in the bound volume. In this case, the Fourth Amendment will be too general to answer the question. The Fourth Amendment simply states that people have the right "to be secure in their persons, houses, papers, and effects, against unreasonable searches and seizures . . . ." Thus, it is important to check for interpretive case law which has defined what constitutes a search. Part of the analysis process is to review the research aids to determine if there is any other relevant information. These aids might lead the researcher to helpful primary or secondary authority.

4. *Pocket Part:* Update the constitutional provision. Although as a practical matter the Constitution has not been amended recently, the researcher should follow the updating procedures. This should be done by reviewing the pocket part in the back of the bound volume. In this problem, there are no changes or additions to the Fourth Amendment.

5. *Supplementary Pamphlet:* Sometimes a quarterly paperbound supplement will be issued if there have been many new cases. If there are so many cases that this is impractical, then a bound volume may be issued. Therefore, the researcher should be aware of these possibilities and look for a supplementary pamphlet.

6. *Update the Provision:* The final update would be to update the provision in *Shepard's Federal Statutes Citations. Shepard's* will update the constitutional provision itself by noting if there have been any amendments to it or if it has been repealed. The researcher can update the provision through *Shepard's* in print or on Lexis Advance or "Key Cite" through WestlawNext.

## [2]  Electronic Version

There are numerous ways to find the Constitution through an electronic search. The text of the Constitution can be found on Lexis Advance as well as WestlawNext. This can be done through using a topic or descriptive word approach. For example, if the researcher wanted to know what the Preamble is to the Constitution and its effect, go to Lexis Advance for its *U.S.C.S.* Code section and click on the Preamble on the Table of Contents. It has the provision, explanatory notes, interpretive cases, and research aids including *Am. Jur.* encyclopedia, and law journal articles. A specific section of the Constitution can be found by citation, subject, or the table of contents.

## [3]  Internet Version

On the Internet, there are many sites where the United States Constitution can be found. For example, the Government Printing Office maintains a site at www.access. gpo.gov/congress/senate/constitution/index.html. It has the text of the Constitution as well as an overview and scholarly commentary. The Constitution with commentary can be found at Findlaw.com/Constitution. Cornell University also has the text of the Constitution at www.law.cornell.edu/constitution/constitution.overview.html.

## D.   FINDING AND UPDATING INTERPRETIVE CASES

The next step in the research process is to find interpretive case law. This may be done in several ways.

## [1]  Print Version

1. *Bound Volume:* Following the research aids section is an Index for the Notes of Decision. Due to the large number of cases that have interpreted the Constitution, a general note index is listed by roman numerals. In addition, a more detailed alphabetical note index precedes each general area. Quick access to the relevant cases is provided through this Index. Thus, the researcher should scan the Index using the key words and phrases that were obtained through the TAPP rule analysis. The most specific word in the analysis should be used. Merely using the

word "dogs," the researcher will find that there is nothing directly on point in the bound volume.

For instance, the most appropriate general index heading for this problem is "XXIII. Conduct Constituting Search or Seizure." Turning to the more specific index and looking under "dog sniffing inspections" at note 1753, there are several on-point cases: *United States v. Place*, a United States Supreme Court decision, *United States v. Goldstein*, an Eleventh Circuit Court of Appeals, *United States v. Beale*, a Ninth Circuit case; and *United States v. Bronstein*, a Second Circuit case.

2. *Pocket Part:* The pocket part should always be checked under the relevant note number. In this example, there is another relevant case, *United States v. Williams*, a United States Court of Appeals for the Fifth Circuit case.

3. *Pamphlet Supplement:* If a quarterly pamphlet has been published, then it should be checked by using the relevant note number. Although the researcher has found an on-point case, all the updating procedures need to be followed. *United States v. Place* directly answers the question. It also demonstrates the research point that ultimately the researcher is looking for a United States Supreme Court case because it is the highest judicial authority.

4. *Update:* The last important step in the research process is to read, analyze, and update any relevant case in the appropriate citator. The researcher can update through *Shepard's* in print or on Lexis Advance or "Key Cite" through WestlawNext.

## [2] Electronic Version

Cases interpreting the Constitution can be found on Lexis Advance as well as WestlawNext. This can be done through case notes that follow the constitutional provision. In the example concerning the Preamble to the Constitution and its effect, the researcher can go to Lexis Advance for the provision. It is followed by explanatory notes, interpretive cases, and research aids including *Am. Jur.* encyclopedia, and law journal articles. A similar process could be used for WestlawNext.

There may be an indirect constitutional problem. This occurs where a statute is deemed constitutional or unconstitutional.

**EXAMPLE #2:** The researcher wants to know if the definition of marriage under the Defense of Marriage Act (DOMA) is constitutional.

DOMA has been codified in more than one place. The definition of marriage is in 1 U.S.C. § 7. In addition, 28 U.S.C. § 1738C concerns documentary evidence such as public act, records, or judicial proceedings for persons of the same-sex that cannot be treated the same as marriage under the law. Thus, the researcher needs to know what section of the Act is relevant.

The Act itself may be located through either the Descriptive Word Method or the Popular Name Table Method. In the *Descriptive Word Index* or the *Popular Name*

*Table* of the *U.S.C.A.*, the Act may be found under "D" for Defense of Marriage Act. Both entries lead the researcher to the provisions listed above. Using the Descriptive Word Method with the word "marriage," the researcher could find 1 U.S.C.A. § 7 under "Definitions" and 28 U.S.C.A. § 1738C under "Same-sex marriages."

The relevant section is 1 U.S.C.A. § 7. Turning to that section, the researcher will find notes of decision. Usually one of the first notes of decision is one for the constitutionality of the provision. In this example, note 1 pertains to constitutionality. In the 2014 cumulative annual pocket part, there is the 2013 United States Supreme Court decision of *United States v. Windsor* determining the federal DOMA law was unconstitutional.

It is always good to check both unofficial codes as different cases may be cited. Because the researcher started in the *U.S.C.A.*, the *U.S.C.S.* should also be checked. Although arranged differently, the lower court decision of *Smelt v. County of Orange* case which was found in the previous chapter of this text can be found. It was not listed in the *U.S.C.A.* notes of decision for either the bound volume or pocket part.

In addition to interpretive case law, each of the unofficial codes refers the researcher to other research aids. This will be discussed in greater detail later. However, suffice it to say at this juncture, references usually differ to correspond to the publisher's various publications. For example, the researcher can find for 1 U.S.C.A. § 7 references to law review articles, the American Digest System, its encyclopedias, and *A.L.R.* In the *U.S.C.S.*, there are references to its encyclopedia, treatises, *A.L.R.*, and law review articles.

# E.  CONSTITUTIONAL INTERPRETATION

There are various views on constitutional interpretation that are beyond the scope of this text. Suffice it to say for now, an understanding and interpretation of the United States Constitution is important. Thus, the question arises as to what primary and secondary sources can be used to interpret the Constitution.

Certainly, the researcher must read and analyze the specific words in the Constitution itself. The plain language of the Constitution is the most important aspect. Beyond the words themselves, the researcher may be faced with interpreting the meaning of a provision or clause of the Constitution. If this were a statute, there may well be some form of legislative history which would be instructive of what the legislators meant. However, there are no legislative history-type materials for the Constitution. The Constitutional Convention did not keep official records of the session. Thus, there may be other sources which may provide some insights. One of the most widely accepted sources is Max Farrand's three-volume set entitled *Records of the Federal Constitution of 1787* that was originally published in 1911 and were the documentary records of the Constitutional Convention.

The researcher may compare the documents of the Continental Congress or the Articles of Confederation. These documents which preceded the adoption of the Constitution may provide valuable insights. Commentaries on the Constitution may be helpful. For example, of the most extensive and authoritative is J. Killian et al., *The*

*Constitution of the United States of America: Analysis and Interpretation* which is published by the Library of Congress. Other publications include L. Levy et al., *Encyclopedia of the American Constitution* and J. Elliot, *The Debates in the Several State Conventions on the Adoption of the Federal Constitution.*

In addition to historical sources, there is a wealth of constitutional commentaries by legal scholars. These include monographs, treatises, encyclopedias, and law review articles. They provide analysis of the constitutional language, how it has been interpreted, and interpretive cases.

Some of these sources are available online. The Library of Congress has one of the most complete collections of U.S. Congressional documents in their original format. It now has an extensive online collection called *A Century of Lawmaking for a New Nation* which has the records and acts of Congress from the Continental Congress and Constitutional Convention through the 43rd Congress. For example, the Library of Congress' website has the full-text of both *Farrand's Records of the Federal Constitution of 1787* and *Elliot's The Debates in the Several State Conventions on the Adoption of the Federal Constitution* at memory.loc.gov/ammem/amlaw/. There is also a founders' series with the thoughts, opinions, and arguments of the founders at http://press-pubs.uchicago.edu/founders.

Westlaw developed a database called LH1776. It contains documents related to the founding of the United States. This includes the Declaration of Independence, the Articles of Confederation, notes on the debates in the Federal Convention of 1787, the *Federalist Papers*, and ratification resolutions of the states. Coverage begins with selected resolutions passed by the First Continental Congress in 1774.

Periodically, United States Supreme Court Justices will expound on constitutional interpretation in their opinions. One such example is Justice Thomas' concurring opinion in *United States v. Lopez*, 514 U.S. 549 (1995). He opines that the case law had "drifted far from the original understanding of the Commerce Clause" and, in the future, decisions should adhere "more faithful[ly] to the original understanding of that Clause." *Id.* at 584. In coming to this conclusion, Justice Thomas analyzed the language of the Constitution, prior case law interpreting that provision, dictionaries from the period and more modern versions, the *Federalist Papers*, letters and pamphlets of the constitutional period, and Elliot's *Debates* (mentioned above as one of the sources). As one commentator stated, this was proper as, "The task of a judge is to find the meanings of constitutional provisions in the intent of their framers and those who originally voted for them." Schmidt, *Clarence Thomas' Use of Historical Sources in* United States v. Lopez, http://www.freerepublic.com/focus/f-chat/1885059/posts.

In summary, when interpreting a constitutional provision, the researcher should:

1. Read and analyzing the text of the Constitution.

2. Examine the historical context and evidence.

3. Read and update cases interpreting that provision, both historical cases and more contemporary ones. The researcher can update the case through *Shepard's* in print or on Lexis Advance or "Key Cite" through WestlawNext.

4. Use other documents, letters, or pamphlets that would explain the context such as the *Federalist Papers* and the *Debates*.

5. Use dictionaries, both from the period and more modern versions.

6. Check treatises that would cite primary authority and expound on the law.

The steps for researching a federal constitutional problem are summarized in the checklist that follows.

---

### CONSTITUTIONAL LAW CHECKLIST

Whether using the print or electronic versions, analyze the facts according to the TAPP rule to determine the key words and phrases.

**Print Version**

1. Find the appropriate constitutional provision in the *U.S.C.A.* or the *U.S.C.S.* by:

   a. The Topic Method; or

   b. The Descriptive Word Method.

2. Read and analyze the appropriate constitutional provision in the bound volumes of the *U.S.C.A.* or the *U.S.C.S.*

3. Review the research aids to determine if there are cross references to other primary or secondary authorities.

4. Update the constitutional provision by:

   a. The annual pocket part;

   b. The quarterly pamphlet supplement, if any; and

   c. *Shepard's Federal Statute Citations.* Updating can be through *Shepard's* in print or on Lexis Advance or "Key Cite" through WestlawNext.

5. Find relevant interpretive case law by:

   a. The Notes of Decision in the *U.S.C.A.* or *U.S.C.S.* in the bound volume;

   b. The digests, if you already have "one good case"; or

   c. Secondary resources such as annotations, treatises, or law review articles if you do not know very much about the subject.

6. Update the case law by:

   a. The annual pocket part;

   b. The quarterly pamphlet supplement, if any; and

   c. The appropriate *Shepard's* citator.

7. Read, analyze, and update all cases through *Shepard's* in print or on Lexis Advance or "Key Cite" through WestlawNext.

**Electronic Version**

1.  Find the appropriate constitutional provision through either a topic or descriptive word approach.

2.  Analyze the provision.

3.  Review the research aids to determine if there are other primary or secondary authorities.

4.  Use the case notes following the provision Lexis Advance or WestlawNext.

5.  Read the case in the appropriate reporter.

6.  Update the case through *Shepard's* on Lexis Advance or "Key Cite" on WestlawNext.

## F.  ADDITIONAL TIPS

1.  Understanding what comprises the founding documents, the reason and authority for constitutional provisions. For example, check the Library of Congress website. It has an extensive online collection called *A Century of Lawmaking for a New Nation* which has the records and acts of Congress from the Continental Congress and Constitutional Convention through the 43rd Congress. The Library of Congress' website has the full-text of both *Farrand's Records of the Federal Constitution of 1787* and *Elliot's The Debates in the Several State Conventions on the Adoption of the Federal Constitution* is available at memory.loc.gov/ammem/amlaw/. There is also a founders' series with the thoughts, opinions, and arguments of the founders at http://press-pubs.uchicago.edu/founders.

2.  Quotations and writings of the founders such as the *Federalist Papers*. For example, the *Federalist Papers* can be found on the Library of Congress site at http://thomas.loc.gov/home/histdox/fedpapers.html.

3.  Discover if there are research guides on various provisions of the Constitution. Duquesne University has various research guides with lists of primary and second resources. For example, there is one generally on the Constitution at http://www.duq.edu/Documents/law/library/_pdf/US-constitution.pdf as well as a more specific one for the First Amendment research guide at http://www.duq.edu/academics/schools/law/law-library/legal-research-guides/constitutional-law-first-amendment.

4.  Discover what treatises are available such as Erwin Chemerinsky's *Constitutional Law: Principles and Policies*; Laurence Tribe's *American Constitutional Law*; John E. Nowak & Ronald D. Rotunda's *Constitutional Law*; Edwin Meese's *Heritage Guide to the Constitution*; Chester Antieau & William J. Rich's *Modern Constitutional Law*.

5.  Review relevant rules, procedures, and practice in constitutional law cases. For example, review the rules for Supreme Court practice for filing briefs on the merits or amicus briefs. These rules are available on the

Supreme Court's website at http://www.supremecourt.gov/ctrules/2013RulesoftheCourt.pdf.

6.  Analyze whether there are any relevant statutes and their interpretive case law. For example, in 1993 Congress enacted the Religious Freedom Restoration Act (RFRA) to prevent laws that substantially burden a person's free exercise of religion which the Constitution protects. Although RFRA was held unconstitutional as applied to the states, it still applies to the federal government. Some states passed State Religious Freedom Restoration Acts that apply to state governments and local municipalities.

7.  Check the National Archives and Records Administration (NARA) available at http://www.archives.gov/exhibits/charters/constitution.html for their section on the Charters of Freedom: Constitution of the United States for access to various documents, articles, biographies of the founders, exhibits, and links to questions and answers.

8.  Find any splits in circuit court decisions in *U.S. Law Week*. This is important for the United States Supreme Court in granting certiorari.

9.  Check Lexis Advance Constitutional Law and Civil Rights Emerging Issues as well as any law reviews on Constitutional Law.

10. There are various blogs on constitutional law such as the SCOTUS blog: Supreme Court of the United States Blog which covers upcoming oral arguments and petitions, Supreme Court Term statistics, and recently decided cases among other materials.

11. Justia provides free Internet access to primary authority as well as legal analysis and commentary. It also provides links to Supreme Court materials.

12. Supreme Court oral arguments. Either as a research tool or in preparation for doing an oral argument at the United States Supreme Court, arguments are recorded and available at http://www.oyez.org/. Oyez features U.S. Supreme Court case summaries, oral arguments, and multimedia.

# Chapter 4

# FEDERAL LEGISLATIVE RESEARCH

## A.  FEDERAL LAW ORGANIZATION

Federal legislative materials are another source of primary authority. Because the common law emphasis has always centered on judicial opinions, the researcher has to fight the tendency to overlook legislation. This is especially true because a growing number of cases involve the interpretation of statutes. In fact, the careful researcher should always ask the following question before beginning any research assignment: Is there a relevant statute?

Researching federal statutes is a complex process because it involves finding and updating the statute. That process, however, is not enough by itself. A statute does not exist in a vacuum. Its validity depends in large part upon the way it is enforced or interpreted by the courts. Any research, then, that involves federal statutes necessarily includes the extra steps of finding interpretive cases. To understand this entire process, it is best to begin with the methods by which statutes are published officially and unofficially.

When the United States Congress passes legislation, it is published officially in three phases, as illustrated by the diagram below:

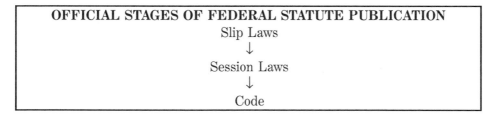

OFFICIAL STAGES OF FEDERAL STATUTE PUBLICATION
Slip Laws
↓
Session Laws
↓
Code

## [1]   Official Sources

The first official stage of publication is a "slip law," an individual pamphlet that contains the text of a single act, similar to a slip opinion. Each slip law is paginated separately and contains a brief summary of its legislative history after the text. Slip laws are issued by their public law number, for example, P.L. 98-128. The first part of the number tells the reader that the law was enacted during the 98th Congress, while the second part of the number represents its chronological sequence of enactment, *i.e.*, the 128th law enacted in the 98th Congress. Slip laws are produced by the United States Government Printing Office and are available in print and electronically on its website (www.gpo.gov/FDsys), or for current legislation (www.Congress.gov) (103rd

Congress (1994)–present).

The second official stage of federal statutory publication is the "session" laws, so designated because they are published at the end of each session of Congress in chronological order by public law number. Variously comprised of as many as six volumes, these materials are known as the *United States Statutes at Large*. Subject and title indices appear at the end of each volume. While slow in publication, this is the authoritative source of federal legislation or *positive law*, which means that the version published in the session laws is legal evidence of statutory language in all United States courts. Electronic access is available through FDsys. The researcher would use the session laws only when there is a dispute over the language of the statute or when it is necessary to know what the statutory language was during a specific time. Furthermore, the researcher should be aware that any subsequent amendments to the statute will be published separately after the session in which it was passed. Therefore, the researcher will have to locate any amendments individually.

The third official stage of publication is in a code. The codification process groups all laws related by subject, includes subsequent amendments, and eliminates those laws which have been repealed. The *United States Code (U.S.C.)* is the official compilation of laws for the United States and is arranged in over 50 titles. A new edition of the Code is issued every six years and supplemented annually with cumulative bound volumes. The Code includes the full text of the statute, followed by a parenthetical reference to the cite of that section in the *Statutes at Large*. There is a general index, a popular name table, and a tables volume which provides cross references to the public law number and the *Statutes at Large* citation. Like other official publications, the *U.S.C.* supplementation is slow, though access to the most up-to-date *U.S.C.* material is through its official website of the Office of Law Revision Counsel (OLRC) (uscode.house.gov). More important to the researcher, however, is the absence of any reference to cases interpreting federal statutes. For this reason alone, the researcher will find the unofficial sources of more value.

## [2]  Unofficial Sources

Since there is no unofficial publication of individual slip laws, the first stage of publication of unofficial materials occurs with session laws. The *United States Code Congressional and Administrative News (U.S.C.C.A.N.)*, published by West, provides on a monthly basis the full text of bills enacted into public law during that time. Also included are selected legislative histories in the form of committee reports for important legislation. LexisNexis provides a similar unofficial session law service entitled the *United States Code Service Advance Service*. These services for statutes are analogous to advance sheets for court reports.

The second stage of unofficial publication is in annotated versions of the *U.S.C.* There are two sets covering this material: The *United States Code Annotated (U.S.C.A.)*, published by West, and the *United States Code Service (U.S.C.S.)*, published by LexisNexis. Both sets provide the language of the U.S. Code statutes, their effective dates, and brief descriptions or annotations of cases interpreting the statutes. Historical references provide citations to the *Statutes at Large* for the law and any amendments, as well as legislative history information. These volumes also have similar update services in the form of annual pocket parts and pamphlet supplements. Because of these similarities, the research processes described below can be applied to either set. Likewise, the search process for Lexis Advance and WestlawNext online accomplish the same tasks.

## B.　FEDERAL LAW LOCATION METHODS

The methods of finding federal statutes are similar to those employed to locate cases, depending upon the information the researcher already has. The simplest method will be described first.

---

**LOOKING FOR A STATUTE?**

Do you have the statute's popular name? If so, use one of the following methods:

1. The OLRC website has a Popular Name tool (http://uscode.house.gov/popularnames/popularnames.htm).

2. The Popular Name Table in the U.S. Code annotated codes, *U.S.C.S.* or *U.S.C.A.*, or *Shepard's Acts and Cases by Popular Names* in print or online through Lexis Advance.

Do you have only the statute's public law number or the *Statutes at Large* volume and page number?

3. Check the tables volumes of the U.S. Code, or the annotated codes in print or online where conversion charts list all public acts by public law number, *Statutes at Large* reference, and the corresponding *U.S.C.* title and section numbers.

If you do *not* have any of the references listed above, use one of the following methods:

4. Descriptive Word Method: Use the U.S. Code's General Index or the annotated codes' General Index in print or online through Lexis Advance or WestlawNext.

5. Topic Method: Select general topics from the titles in the U.S. Code and go to the relevant title's index in print in the *U.S.C.S.* or *U.S.C.A.* online through Lexis Advance or WestlawNext.

---

## [1]　Popular Name Method

If the researcher has only the popular name of a law and wants to locate the legislation, the simplest technique for finding the statute is to go to *Shepard's Acts and Cases by Popular Name*, or the *Popular Name Table* in the *U.S.C.S.* or *U.S.C.A.* in print or online, which lists only those federal statutes with popular names in alphabetical order. Here is an illustration.

**EXAMPLE:** Assume that the federal statute's popular name is the Lanham Act. Use the following steps:

1. Bound Volume: Go to the volume of the *Shepard's Acts and Cases by Popular Name*, *U.S.C.S.* or *U.S.C.A.* containing the *Popular Name Table* or the electronic version in these sources. Check by alphabetical designation. In this example, you would look under "L" for "Lanham Act."

2. Statute Volume: When you find the Lanham Act, the citation will tell you to consult Title 15 Section 1501 *et seq.* Look up the statute in the appropriate annotated code, in print or online.

## [2]  Tables Method

A quick way to locate federal legislation involves the tables volumes of the *U.S.C.S.* and *U.S.C.A.* or scroll down to the "Tables" tab online for *U.S.C.S.* or *U.S.C.A.* When the researcher knows the public law number or has only the *Statutes at Large* cite, the tables in the annotated codes provide cross references to the *U.S.C.* Here is a problem that illustrates this process.

**EXAMPLE:** The researcher knows that the Public Law Number is 112-190 and wants to find the U.S. Code title and section. Use the following steps:

1. Bound Volume: Go to the tables volume in the *U.S.C.S.* or *U.S.C.A.* or consult the "Tables" tab for the electronic *U.S.C.S.* or *U.S.C.A.* Public laws are listed there in numerical order by session of Congress. Locate the 112th Congress and then Public Law Number 112-190. The *Statutes at Large* cite and the *U.S.C.* title and section number will be listed there. For this problem, Title 15 Section 1125 is the appropriate title and section.

2. Cumulative Supplement: Check any supplements to the bound volume, such as a pocket part or a paper supplement or note the currentness or effective date on Lexis Advance or WestlawNext.

There are two subject matter methods of finding a statute. One problem will be used to demonstrate both of these methods.

**EXAMPLE:** A popular women's shoe designer is known for the distinctive red outsoles on all of his high-heeled shoes. Another designer is marketing a monochrome red shoe with a red outsole. Has a trademark infringement occurred?

## [3]  Topic Method

One way to find a federal statute is by the Topic Method. A list of the fifty plus titles in the *U.S.C.* is published in the front of each volume of the unofficial annotated codes, or listed online through Lexis Advance or WestlawNext. As soon as the researcher becomes familiar with the code's organization, it is possible to select the correct title by glancing through these topics. The topic method for locating federal statutes is simpler than using the same procedure to find cases because there are only fifty plus topics in the code, compared to 435 in the digests.

Because this is a "trademark" issue, the researcher might conclude that no title in the *U.S.C.* would apply! None of the titles specifically references "trademark," so familiarity with "Commerce and Trade" would be necessary to know that this title addresses trademark legislation in Chapter 22.

## [4]   Descriptive Word Method

The Descriptive Word Method, once again, is the most common means of locating a federal statute when the researcher has a fact situation with no popular name or immediately obvious topic that relates to one of the fifty plus code titles. The process should begin with an analysis of the facts according to the TAPP rule.

Using the descriptive word method, analyze the facts according to the TAPP rule, which is the common form of analysis for legislative materials. Some words that might be used in this analysis are:

| | |
|---|---|
| Things: | shoes, shoe soles, design |
| Acts: | trademark infringement |
| Persons: | designer |

1.  Index Bound Volume: The researcher should go to the General Index of the *U.S.C.S.* or the *U.S.C.A.*, in print or electronic format. In either index the words "shoes," and "shoe soles" lack references to trademark or cross-reference "footwear" without trademark references. Likewise, there are no trademark cites under "design" or "designer." The broadest topic "trademarks" will provide access to Title 15 "infringement" remedies generally at Sections 1114 *et seq.*

2.  Print Index Pocket Part: In the *U.S.C.S.* and *U.S.C.A.*, the General Index is paperbound so there will be no pocket part.

3.  Read and Analyze the Provision in the Bound Volume: Title 15 Section 1114 *et seq.* contains the information needed to determine trademark infringement. Read the language of the statute carefully and make note of the historical material directly following its language. Included there will be the effective date of the statute. This is important because the researcher must be sure to locate the provision in effect at the time of the legal dispute. Subsequent changes in the law may not be pertinent to the dispute. Citations to legislative history will also be noted, as well as cross references to the publishers' other sources, such as encyclopedias and form books. Electronic format of *U.S.C.S.* and *U.S.C.A.* also provides citations to any law review articles as well as links to appellate briefs, if any, on point.

## C. FINDING AND UPDATING A FEDERAL LAW

### [1] Print Version

To see if the statute is still current or if it has been amended or repealed, follow the steps below.

1. Pocket Part: Check the cumulative annual pocket part found at the back of the *U.S.C.S.* or *U.S.C.A.* bound volume by title and section number.

2. Supplementary Pamphlet: If there is a cumulative supplementary pamphlet, check for the relevant title and section number.

3. Session Laws: Consult the unofficial session laws. This will tell you whether there has been any change during the current legislative session. Both unofficial session law services for *U.S.C.S.* and *U.S.C.A.* have cumulative tables of code sections amended or repealed. Locate the most recent issue of the monthly publications and check the title and section number of the act.

4. Update: Federal statutes should be Shepardized in a manner similar to cases, through *Shepard's Federal Statute Citations* by title and section number. Citations are given to cases that have ruled on or discussed the statute. Most important to this process are the capital letters "C" and "U" which may appear to the left of a case citation. These letters indicate that a court has found the statute constitutional or unconstitutional. Be sure to check all volumes and supplements to *Shepard's* where the statute may appear if updating in hard copy.

### [2] Electronic Version

1. Locate the relevant federal statute using the General Index in *U.S.C.S.* on Lexis Advance or *U.S.C.A.* on WestlawNext. Note the effectiveness date and legislative history references. Citations to law review articles, as well as links to appellate briefs, if any, are available.

2. *U.S.C.S.* and *U.S.C.A.* maintain currency often within a month of the current date.

3. Update the statute through *Shepard's* on Lexis Advance or KeyCite on WestlawNext.

### [3] Internet Version

Federal statutes are accessible through the U.S. Code's official website in the Office of Law Revision Council (OLRC) (uscode.house.gov) or FDsys (gpo.gov/fdsys/browse/collectionUSCode). These sources provide no access to interpretive opinions. Fastcase and Casemaker also provide access to federal statutes.

## D.   FINDING AND UPDATING INTERPRETIVE CASES

The next task is to find a case on point that interprets the statute. Judicial interpretations can be found in the following manner.

### [1]   Print Version

1. Bound Volume: Following the statutory language in the bound volume of the *U.S.C.S.* or *U.S.C.A.* annotated codes are Notes of Decisions which describe in short paragraphs those cases interpreting the statute. These Notes of Decisions are organized under subject headings and paragraph numbers.

2. Pocket Part: To locate more recent decisions, read the relevant Notes of Decisions located by the appropriate paragraph number in the pocket part to find a case on point.

3. Supplementary Pamphlet: Check each pamphlet update by the same process.

4. Advance Sheets: Go to the *Cumulative Table of Statutes Construed* in the latest advance sheets for West's *Supreme Court Reporter, Federal Reporter,* and *Federal Supplement.* These tables will cite federal cases interpreting the statute which have been published in the reporter system but which have not yet been included in either the pocket part or a supplementary pamphlet.

5. Update: Relevant cases should be Shepardized in the *Shepard's* corresponding to the reporter where the case is reported.

### [2]   Electronic Version

1. Notes of Decisions follow the statutory language in the *U.S.C.S.* and *U.S.C.A.* electronic versions. These notes are organized under subject headings and paragraph numbers.

2. Another means to locate cases interpreting red sole shoes as a trademark violation would be through a Lexis Advance or WestlawNext word search such as "trademark infringement red sole shoes." That process could lead directly to a Second Circuit case on point with internal references to applicable provisions within Title 15.

3. Update all relevant decisions through *Shepard's* on Lexis Advance or KeyCite on WestlawNext.

### [3]   Internet Version

1. Because official sources provide no citations to cases interpreting federal laws, free access to such decisions is available only when the researcher has a case citation through a specific federal court's website, such as supremecourt.gov, or for federal circuit court opinions, uscourts.gov. There is no update function with these sources.

2. Fastcase provides cases interpreting federal laws updated through its Bad Law Bot feature, and Casemaker offers a similar service through its Statute Annotator, which shows how courts construe the law. Any such interpretive case should be updated through Casecheck+.

---

## LEGISLATIVE RESEARCH CHECKLIST

Analyze the fact situation according to the TAPP rule.

**Print Version:**

1. Locate the relevant statute by using:

   a. *Shepard's Acts and Cases by Popular Name* in print or the annotated code's *Popular Name Table* in the General Index;

   b. The tables in the annotated codes in print for the conversion charts;

   c. The Descriptive Word Method in the annotated code's General Index;

   d. The Topic Method in the fifty plus titles of the annotated code in print.

2. Read the statute, looking for particular language and any reference to legislative history.

3. Update the statute itself by:

   a. The pocket part;

   b. The supplementary pamphlet;

   c. The unofficial session laws in *U.S.C.S.* or *U.S.C.C.A.N.*; and

   d. Updating the statute in *Shepard's Federal Statute Citations*.

4. Find interpretive cases:

   a. Check the Notes of Decisions in the bound volume;

   b. Check the Notes of Decisions in the pocket part;

   c. Check the Notes of Decisions in the supplementary pamphlet;

   d. Check the cumulative Tables of Statutes Construed in the advance sheets of all federal court reporters; and

   e. Update all relevant cases in the appropriate *Shepard's*.

**Electronic Version:**

1. Locate the relevant statute by using:

   a. *Shepard's Acts and Cases by Popular Name* on Lexis Advance or the WestlawNext *Popular Name Table*;

   b. The *U.S.C.S.* or *U.S.C.A.* conversion tables in the online annotated codes;

   c. The Descriptive Word Method in the online statutes;

   d. The Topic Method in the annotated online statutes.

2. Read the relevant provision, looking for the effectiveness date and legislative history reference.

3. Update the statute by checking the currency status designation and Shepardize on Lexis Advance or KeyCite on WestlawNext.

4. Find interpretive cases directly through the links located with the statutory language on Lexis Advance or WestlawNext.

5. Update the cases through *Shepard's* on Lexis Advance or KeyCite on WestlawNext.

**Internet Version:**

Access to current U.S. Code material is available at its official website in the Office of Law Revision Council (OLRC) (uscode.house.gov) or FDsys (gpo. gov/fdsys/browse/collectionUSCode). These sources provide no access to interpretive opinions. Fastcase and Casemaker also provide access to federal laws and interpretive cases.

## E. FEDERAL LEGISLATIVE HISTORY

The legislative history of federal statutes can be important to the researcher for two main reasons. First, the status of pending legislation may need to be traced, or for laws already enacted, it may be necessary to determine the legislative intent of an act. Second, courts use legislative intent to determine the meaning of vague language in a statute, the reason for any change in a statute, or for a statement of the law's purpose. Because so many sources must be consulted, researching legislative history can be a very complex process. The most important starting point is the date of the law's enactment. That date enables the researcher to navigate through official and unofficial sources, depending on the dates of the source's coverage.

A complete legislative history involves various elements related to the process by which a bill becomes law. As the detailed chart at the end of this section indicates, relevant information may be obtained at various levels of the legislative process. In addition, some elements of a legislative history carry more weight than others and are summarized briefly below in order of importance:

1. *Committee Reports.* These are the most important items of a legislative history. Issued when a bill is reported out of either House, Senate, or Conference Committee, committee reports often contain the bill itself, an analysis of its content and its purpose, any suggested changes, as well as the reasons for the committee's specific proposals. Minority reports, if any, are also included.

2. *Bills.* The proposed legislation itself is also important in a legislative history. When a bill is introduced into the House or Senate, it is assigned a number. This number identifies the bill within that particular chamber. If an identical bill is submitted to both houses, a separate number will be assigned by each chamber. The bill number remains the same for a session of Congress. If the bill does not pass by the end of the session,

then it must be resubmitted in the next session, at which time new numbers will be assigned. A bill may be amended or changed at any time during the legislative process. Each change may be important to the history of the bill as a reflection of congressional intent.

3. *Congressional Debates.* Floor discussion of proposed legislation can occur at any time in the enactment process, although generally debates take place after a bill has been reported out of committee. These debates sometimes focus on the intent of Congress; however, because individual members of Congress can manipulate these proceedings in a manner calculated to sway a court's interpretation of legislative intent, the importance of congressional debates is reduced.

4. *Hearings.* Senate and House committees may hold hearings to study pending legislation. Such hearings usually include testimony from non-legislators, such as experts and concerned citizens. As a result, their importance for the purposes of determining legislative intent is reduced. Moreover, not all committee hearings are published.

## [1]  Official Sources

Most elements of a legislative history are available through official sources. Committee Reports are numbered and published individually. These reports are listed in the *Monthly Catalog of U.S. Government Publications.* The reports are also published in a bound series of House and Senate documents called the *Serial Set* and are available through the FDsys Advanced search page. Proposed bills are also published individually and may be obtained from Congress, from libraries that are designated federal depositories or through an online source such as the Library of Congress website available at Congress.gov. Congressional debates are published in the *Congressional Record,* which appear daily while Congress is in session. The daily hard copy issues are then cumulated into an annual bound volume. While the *Congressional Record* attempts to record debate verbatim, legislators may revise their remarks. These revisions appear in the Appendix for each daily issue but not in the annual bound volumes. The *Congressional Record* is indexed every two weeks by title of legislation, subject matter, and legislator's name. These indices are not, however, cumulated until the annual bound volume appears. The permanent edition of the Congressional Record is available electronically through Congress.gov back to 1989, FDsys back to 1994, ProQuest Congressional Record Permanent Digital Collection, and HeinOnline.

## [2]   Unofficial Sources

Unofficial publications also provide access to the elements of a legislative history. A good starting point is Johnson's *Sources of Compiled Legislative Histories*, also available at Heinonline, which lists major compilations of legislative history by publisher, subject matter, and public law number. The *Congressional Information Service* (C.I.S.), available through ProQuest, is the unofficial source that provides the most complete coverage of legislative history sources. Commenced in 1970, this digital subscription service issues a monthly index of committee reports, hearings, and documents. These indices are cumulated quarterly and annually. Another good feature of this service is the abstracts provided for these materials. There is also a status table for pending legislation. To coordinate with the indices, C.I.S. instituted a microfiche service, also begun in 1970, offering the full text of all documents in the index volumes. Complete legislative histories, updated monthly, are available from 1999–present, and abbreviated legislature histories are available from 1984–1998. Another good starting point is the Law Librarians Society of Washington D.C.'s website, llsdc.org. Click on the Legislative Sourcebook link and drill down to "Legislative Histories of U.S. Laws on the Internet: Commercial Sources" and "Legislative Histories of Selected U.S. Laws on the Internet: Free Sources" for explanations of free and fee-based materials.

Another unofficial print publication that provides quick access to the status of pending legislation is the *Congressional Index* published by Wolters Kluwer. Issued in two volumes, the set provides tables arranged by subject matter, sponsors' names, and status tables, with references to hearings and committee reports. Updated weekly, the service is an excellent reference to locate quickly a bill's status. The set, however, does not provide the text of committee reports, bills, hearings, or debates. The Library of Congress website at Congress.gov is a good source of legislative history information for bills pending in Congress. The site includes the text of bills and the bills' status, as well as actions, sponsors, committees, and related bills.

An unofficial source of more limited use is *U.S.C.C.A.N.*, which selectively publishes some committee reports, as well as a legislative history table of laws enacted. Pending legislation, however, is omitted and no abstracts are provided. This material is available in hard copy and in electronic format through WestlawNext. Lexis Advance also provides selected legislative history in electronic format.

## F.  LEGISLATIVE HISTORY LOCATION METHODS

### LOOKING FOR FEDERAL LEGISLATIVE HISTORY?

Do you need the status of pending legislation? If so, use the following:

1. *Congressional Index* status table: Arranged by House or Senate bill number. This source does not provide bill texts, committee reports, hearings, or debates.

2. Library of Congress website at Congress.gov or fdsys/search/advanced/ advsearchpage. Arranged by congressional session and accessible with House or Senate bill number or subject, or Lexis Advance, or WestlawNext, both of which include full text of bills.

Do you need the legislative history of a statute already enacted? If so, use the following:

3. ProQuest's digital legislative history from 1999–present: Check the legislative history arranged by public law number, ProQuest Congressional online subscription.

4. Lexis Advance and WestlawNext provide selected legislative history materials for federal statutes through the links provided with the statutory language.

## [1]  Legislative History of Pending Federal Legislation

The *Congressional Index* status table is updated weekly and provides information on pending legislation. Here is an illustration:

**EXAMPLE:** Locate the status of a bill involving non-disparagement of Native Americans in trademarks submitted in the 113th Congress.

1. Subject Index: Find the bill number in Volume 1 by looking in the Subject Index. A House or Senate Bill number, if any, will be listed there.

2. Status Table: There is a separate status table for House and Senate bills, arranged in chronological order by bill number. Check the appropriate table accordingly.

3. Text of Proposed Law: Congress.gov provides the text of the bill(s), actions, amendments, sponsors, committees, and related bills as does FDsys. The full text of congressional bills is available on Lexis Advance and WestlawNext.

## [2]  Legislative History of Federal Statutes

Assume that the statute has already been enacted and the researcher has the public law number and date of passage. Below is a problem to illustrate the process.

**EXAMPLE:** While researching the red shoe sole trademark problem earlier in the chapter, you find a reference for Title 15 § 1114's legislative history in

House Report No. 109-33(1), which you found in the *U.S.C.S.* or *U.S.C.A.* in print or online. Use the following steps:

1. *U.S.C.S.* or *U.S.C.A.* electronic access to legislative history links to this Report.

2. With the public law number, go to ProQuest electronic subscription service and locate Public Law No. 109-9 where the House Report will be listed.

3. Copies of the law itself, the reports, and hearings can be obtained through ProQuest's digital or C.I.S. microfiche collection or individually through official sources. Debate material must be located directly from the *Congressional Record.* Lexis Advance and WestlawNext provide selected legislative history materials, including links to this House Report, the Congressional Record, testimony to various House or Senate Committees, and Presidential messages.

---

### FEDERAL LEGISLATIVE HISTORY CHECKLIST

1. Analyze the fact situation to determine whether you need the status of pending legislation or the history of a law already passed.

2. Locate the relevant material for pending legislation by using the hard copy *Congressional Index* from Wolters Kluwer or the Library of Congress website at Congress.gov.

3. Find legislative history of a law already passed by:

   a. Checking the legislative history notes in *U.S.C.S.* or *U.S.C.A.* in print or online, following the language of the statute. Note the date the change was made and the public law number; check the history references for the law and examine any links provided to House and Senate Reports, Congressional Record materials, testimony to House or Senate Committees, and Presidential messages, if any;

   b. Checking ProQuest Congressional's electronic Legislative Histories;

   c. Obtaining all documents listed from ProQuest Congressional electronic files, if available or, if not, from official sources such as FDsys or Congress.gov.

## FEDERAL LEGISLATIVE HISTORY CHART

| Legislative Process | Possible Documents | How to Find |
|---|---|---|
| 1. Preliminary Matters | Hearings may be held prior to the introduction of a bill. The problem may be discussed during several Congressional sessions. | Locate through:<br>a. Congress.gov;<br>b. FDsys;<br>c. House.gov;<br>d. Senate.gov;<br>e. Lexis Advance;<br>f. WestlawNext; and<br>g. ProQuest Congressional. |
| 2. Presidential Statements | Presidential message or a memo from an executive agency. These reveal the purpose of the legislation and the intent of the drafters. Example: President's State of the Union Addresas. | Locate through:<br>a. *Congressional Record;*<br>b. *Daily/Weekly Compilation of Presidential Documents;*<br>c. House & Senate Journals; or<br>d. House & Senate Documents. |
| 3. Bill is introduced | Amendments to the bill are helpful in determining legislative intent. Likewise, the inclusion or deletion of particular language aids in determining legislative intent. | Locate through:<br>a. Library of Congress website Congress.gov; or<br>b. on microfiche at libraries that subscribe to a microfiche service or are a federal depository; or<br>c. ProQuest Congressional. |
| 4. Referred to a Committee | Committee prints of the bill. | |
| 5. Hearings | May be held to investigate the problem and to elicit the views of individuals or groups who may be expert or lay witnesses. May publish a transcript of testimony and exhibits. Criticized because it contains the views of non-legislators. But it is helpful because it contains information regarding *why* Congress adopted or rejected certain language. | Locate through:<br>a. Library of Congress website Congress.gov.<br>b. CCH *Congressional Index;*<br>c. Committee websites<br>d. ProQuest Congressional Hearings Digital Collection |

| | | | |
|---|---|---|---|
| 6. | Committee Reports | This is one of the most valuable sources because they contain an analysis of the bill's content and intent, the committee's recommendations and reasoning, minority report, etc. | Locate through:<br>  a.  Library of Congress website Congress.gov;<br>  b.  ProQuest U.S. Serial Set Digital Collection;<br>  c.  Lexis Advance and WestlawNext beginning in 1990;<br>  d.  United States Congress Serial Set in print or ProQuest's U.S. Serial Set Digital Collection.<br>  e.  U.S.C.C.A.N. in hard copy of selected reports. |
| 7. | Congressional Debates | Arguments for or against the bill or amendments are made or explanations of unclear portions may be stated. This source of legislative history has been criticized. | Locate through:<br>  (1)  The daily edition is available at the Library of Congress website Congress.gov as well as FDsys.<br>  (2)  Lexis Advance and WestlawNext coverage begins with 1985. |
| 8. | Final vote | An "engrossed bill," the final draft copy, is presented for vote. | Action is recorded in the *Congressional Record.* See #7. |
| 9. | Sent to other house | Generally the same procedure as #4 through #8. | Generally the same documents and publications as #4 through #8. |
| 10. | Referred to a Conference Committee | If the House & Senate bills do not contain the same language, then a conference committee will review them to try and reconcile any differences. A conference report may be issued. | Published the same as a committee report described in #6. |
| 11. | Passage by the second house | An "enrolled bill," one that is signed by the Speaker of the House or the President of the Senate, is sent to the President. | Available at Library of Congress website Congress.gov beginning with 101 Congress. |
| 12. | Presidential action | The President may veto or approve the bill and include a statement as to his reasoning. | Locate through:<br>  Available in Daily/Weekly Compilation of Presidential Documents in FDsys. |

## G.  ADDITIONAL TIPS

1.  Lexis Advance and WestlawNext provide access to federal forms for pleadings and jury instructions, as well as relevant appellate briefs.

2.  Consider searching electronic references to the business sources, as well as information about their executives, involved in federal statutory disputes.

3.  Lexis Advance and WestlawNext provide the means to search judges' names, as well as trademark cases they may have published.

4.  Secondary sources, such as law review articles, treatises, encyclopedia or *A.L.R.* annotations are available tools for background information and additional citations to primary sources and are accessible through Lexis Advance and WetlawNext.

5.  Government websites relevant to the issue may provide important information on application processes, application forms and deadlines, as well as agency decisions, if any, on point.

# Chapter 5

# FEDERAL ADMINISTRATIVE RESEARCH

## A. ADMINISTRATIVE LAW ORGANIZATION

The administrative function of the federal government has by tradition been relegated to a status below that of judicial decisions and federal statutes. This is due in large measure to the fact that the agencies responsible for administering federal laws derive their authority through delegation of power from either the President or Congress. However, the growth of federal authority, in the form of increasingly complex federal statutes and executive functions, has made it necessary for anyone doing legal research to understand that whenever specific implementation of the law is at issue, it is necessary to find and update all relevant administrative materials.

These materials take many forms, depending upon their purpose. The President's office, for example, issues executive orders and proclamations that affect the function and organization of administrative agencies. Those agencies issue licenses, orders, opinions, decisions, and, probably most important, rules and regulations that articulate the means by which federal laws are enforced. Because federal rules and regulations generally have the greatest impact of all administrative functions, this chapter will focus on the complex process of how they are published and updated. Like federal statutes, these rules and regulations do not exist in a vacuum, and their enforcement depends upon the federal courts and administrative agencies for interpretation. All research into federal rules and regulations will, as a result, include the extra steps of finding any interpretive cases. To explain this process, it is best to begin with the official method by which federal rules and regulations are published.

### [1] Official Sources

In order for any federal rule or regulation to take effect, it must first be published in the *Federal Register.* Produced by the Government Printing Office, the *Federal Register* is issued daily except for Saturday, Sunday, and holidays. Analogous to the *United States Statutes at Large*, it contains rules and regulations ultimately arranged by the title and part numbers of the *Code of Federal Regulations (C.F.R.)*, which will be discussed below. Each issue of the *Federal Register* contains an index of that day's changes in rules and regulations, as well as a cumulative list of all changes from the beginning of the month forward to that day. At the end of each month a separate pamphlet index appears, followed ultimately by an annual index. Daily issues of the *Federal Register* are available in print and online through the Government Printing Office Federal Digital System known as FDsys (fdsys/browse/collection).

After a rule or regulation appears in the *Federal Register*, it is incorporated into the *C.F.R.*, arranged in 50 titles similar, but not identical to, the *U.S.C.* Each title is divided into chapters which usually bear the name of the issuing agency. Each chapter is further subdivided into parts covering specific regulatory areas. An index, issued annually, is contained in a separate volume entitled *C.F.R. Index and Finding Aids*, which has been criticized as too general in its classification of subject terms. Published annually, the *C.F.R.* is issued at quarterly intervals as follows:

Titles 1 through 16 published as of January 1st

Titles 17 through 27 published as of April 1st

Titles 28 through 41 published as of July 1st

Titles 42 through 50 published as of October 1st

Each title contains all regulations still in force, incorporating those that took effect during the preceding 12 months and deleting those revoked. The *C.F.R.* is accessible in print and online through FDsys by selecting the Code of Federal Regulations from the Collections menu of the Advanced Search page (gpo.gov.fdsys/browse/collection). The GPO offers an unofficial version of the *C.F.R.* known as the e-CFR (http://www. ecfr.gov), also accessible through FDsys with the *C.F.R.* link. The value of this tool is its daily update feature, eliminating the cumbersome hard copy update process.

An official guide to the organization of federal agencies is produced by the Office of the Federal Register and entitled the *United States Government Manual*. Issued annually, it explains how agencies function and provides names and addresses of Washington and regional offices as well as agency websites. Thus, it can be a useful starting point if the researcher does not know anything about the relevant agency. The U.S. Government Manual is available at usgovernmentmanual.gov or at FDsys by choosing Government Manual from Available Collections drop-down menu at the Advanced Search page or another official website usa.gov/Agencies.shtml, which provides an alphabetical list of agencies.

## [2]  Unofficial Sources

There is no unofficial source that prints all federal rules and regulations.

For hard copy unofficial access into the *C.F.R.*, Lexis Advance provides the *C.F.R. Index and Finding Aids* volume as a supplement to the *U.S.C.S.* West's *Code of Federal Regulations General Index* is an annual multi-volume paperbound set with over 700,000 term references into *C.F.R.* sections.

In addition, unofficial loose leaf services through hard copy or electronic access provide access to specific rules and regulations of individual agencies, such as the *Employment Practices Guide* by Commerce Clearing House.

Lexis Advance and WestlawNext provide access to the *Federal Register* and the *C.F.R.* Fastcase provides access to the *C.F.R.* and the *Federal Register* through a link to GPO. Casemaker includes the *C.F.R.* in its federal library.

## B.   FEDERAL RULE AND REGULATION LOCATION METHODS

The methods of finding federal rules and regulations are similar to those used to locate federal statutes, depending on what information the researcher possesses. The simplest method will be described first.

---

**LOOKING FOR A FEDERAL RULE OR REGULATION?**

Do you have the enabling legislation? If so, use the following method:

1. *C.F.R. Index and Finding Aids* volume: Lists federal statutes in the *Parallel Table of Authorities* by title and section numbers matched with the title and part numbers to corresponding rules and regulations. This table is also available through the FDsys Code of Federal Regulations library (fdsys/browse/collection/cfr).

If you do not have the enabling legislation, use one of the following methods:

2. Descriptive Word Method: Information arranged according to subject matter in the *C.F.R. Index and Finding Aids* volume or Advanced Search through the FDsys website. Lexis Advance and WestlawNext also provide access to the *C.F.R.* through this method.

3. Topic Method: Information arranged according to the 50 topics or titles in the *C.F.R.* Review all topics either through FDsys *C.F.R.* or e-CFR and select the title/topic relevant to the search. Lexis Advance and West-lawNext also provide the 50 topics or titles of the *C.F.R.* for browsing.

4. Agency Method: Agencies arranged in alphabetical order in the *C.F.R. Index and Finding Aids* volume, through the U.S. Government Manual in hard copy or online (usgovernmentmanual.gov) or through another governmental website (usa.gov/Agencies.shtml), which provides an alphabetical list.

---

## [1]   Enabling Legislation Method

If the researcher only has the enabling legislation, *i.e.*, the federal statute that gives the agency issuing the rule or regulation its authority to do so, the simplest technique for finding the rule or regulation is to go to the most recent annual index in the *C.F.R.* or FDsys *C.F.R.* library and check the *Parallel Table of Authorities*. Here is an illustration:

> **EXAMPLE:** Assume that you need to locate any federal rules and regulations for submitting a trademark application. You have only the title and section number of the statute authorizing these regulations, in this instance 15 U.S.C. § 1501 *et seq.* Use the following steps:
>
> 1. *Index Volume:* Go to the annual *C.F.R. Index and Finding Aids* volume and locate the parallel table of authorities. This table provides cross reference by *U.S. Code* title and section number, listed in numerical order, into any

applicable *C.F.R.* title and section number. Another hard copy alternative is the Parallel Table of Authorities in the Index and Finding Aids to Code of Federal Regulations volume in LexisNexis's United States Code Service (*U.S.C.S.*). For electronic access, consult e-CFR using the "___ U.S. ___" format switched to the pull-down menu "Authority" field. On Lexis Advance or WestlawNext, locate the U.S. Code section in the *C.F.R.* database.

2. *Bound Volume:* When you check the *Parallel Table of Authorities* under Title 15, section 1051, there will be a reference to 37 C.F.R. § 2.32 addressing requirements for a complete application. Go to that title and read the regulations.

## [2]  Descriptive Word Method

### [a]  Print Version

The most common means of locating a federal rule or regulation is the descriptive word method. In analyzing the facts, the researcher should pay particular attention to the date of the dispute. The rule or regulation in effect at the time that the legal dispute arose must be located. This means that if a 2010 rule or regulation is at issue, the researcher would begin the descriptive word process in the index for that year. Here is a problem that illustrates this process:

**EXAMPLE:** What are the current requirements to complete a trademark application?

Using the TAPP rule, the reader might employ the following words or phrases:

|          |            |
|----------|------------|
| Things:  | trademark  |
| Acts:    | application |
| Persons: | N/A        |
| Places:  | N/A        |

"Trademarks" lists a category for "Practice rules in trademark cases." Title 37, encompassing Patents, Trademarks and Copyright Regulations, § 2.32 covers trademark applications.

Once the researcher has located the appropriate title and part number in the index volume, the next step is to go to the appropriate title and part in C.F.R. Title 37, Patents, Trademarks and Copyright Regulations, which appears annually on July 1. Read through part 2.32. Note there the cross reference to the enabling legislation that provides the authority for these rules and regulations.

### [b]  Electronic Version

Lexis Advance and WestlawNext provide access to the *C.F.R.* through this method.

### [c]   Internet Version

Access through the Advanced Search process (gpo.gov.fdsys/browse/collection) or the unofficial version know as the e-CFR (ecfr.gov) provides the same coverage. Fastcase and Casemaker also offer *C.F.R.* access.

### [3]   Topic Method

A less reliable way to find a federal rule or regulation is the topic method. If the researcher is familiar with the 50 titles in the *C.F.R.*, it is possible to select the correct topic by glancing through each title's subject.

The trademark application issue may be used to demonstrate the topic method. Because the issue centers around trademarks, the most obvious choice would be Title 37, "Patents, Trademarks and Copyright." This title provides the rules and regulations governing trademarks. A complicating factor is the absence of individual indices within each title, which forces the reader to scan all subdivisions of every topic to locate the relevant part. If the researcher nevertheless were to locate the appropriate provision, the remainder of the research and update process set out below would be identical to that used with the descriptive word method.

### [4]   Agency Method

The *C.F.R. Index and Finding Aids* volume lists agencies and where materials for a specific agency can be found. That section of the Index is entitled "Alphabetical List of Agencies Appearing in the C.F.R." Because the references are to a general code title, this method is used if the researcher is looking for the agency's body of regulations or wants to combine this method with the topic method. The U.S. Government Manual in hard copy or online (usgovernmentmanual.gov) or usa.gov/Agencies.shtml provides another way to find all federal agencies and their individual websites. The trademark application regulations can be easily located by scanning the titles to find Title 37, "Patents, Trademarks and Copyright."

## C.   UPDATING FEDERAL RULES AND REGULATIONS

Once you have located and read the rule or regulation applicable to the problem, the next step is to determine whether any changes have occurred since the publication date listed on the cover of the *C.F.R.* volume. Follow the steps below.

### [1]   Print Version

1.  *Supplementary Pamphlet:* Check the most recent print issue of the monthly *C.F.R. List of Sections Affected (L.S.A.).* Arranged by title and section number, this publication will cite to a page in the *Federal Register* if any change has occurred to Title 37, Part 2.32.

2.  *Federal Register:* Locate the most recent print issue of the daily *Federal Register.* At the end of each issue is a cumulative list of sections affected for the month arranged by title and part number. If a change has

occurred, its page number in the *Federal Register* is given. Because the *Federal Register* is published and distributed so quickly, you should be able to update with this source to within a week of the current date.

## [2]   Electronic Version

Lexis Advance and WestlawNext maintain ongoing updates to the *C.F.R.* current within a day or two.

## [3]   Internet Version

The e-CFR maintains ongoing updates current within a couple of days.

## D.   FINDING AND UPDATING INTERPRETIVE CASES

Once you have located and updated a federal rule or regulation, there are three ways of finding interpretive cases:

## [1]   Print Version

1. *Shepard's:* Federal rules and regulations should be Shepardized in a manner similar to federal statutes, *i.e.*, by title and part number. The purpose of Shepardizing a rule or regulation is to locate interpretive cases, since case annotations are lacking in both the *C.F.R.* and the *Federal Register. Shepard's Code of Federal Regulations Citations* is a source for finding judicial treatment of federal rules and regulations. It does not, however, indicate whether an agency has repealed or deleted a rule or regulation. Be sure to check all volumes and supplements to the *Shepard's C.F.R. Citations.*

2. *Federal Agency Publications:* At least 30 federal agencies render and publish official opinions. Because these decisions are issued in official reports, publication is slow. Commercial loose leaf services are also available in print as well as selected agency decisions.

3. *Unofficial Reporters:* There is no single source that publishes decisions from all administrative agencies or all judicial interpretations of federal rules and regulations. There are, however, unofficial reports focusing on specific subject areas. For example, loose leaf services, such as the Bureau of National Affairs *Labor Relations Reference Manual,* offer coverage of agency and federal court decisions, as well as frequent updates. Some of these unofficial sets provide their own citators. Otherwise, these cases should be Shepardized in the appropriate sets.

## [2]  Electronic Version

Lexis Advance and WestlawNext provide access to opinions interpreting federal regulations through citing references by *C.F.R.* Title and Section number. Update any decision located through *Shepard's* on Lexis Advance of KeyCite on WestlawNext.

## [3]  Internet Version

Access to federal agency opinions is available at the relevant agency websites. Consult Casemaker and Fastcase coverage of selected agency opinions.

---

### FEDERAL RULES AND REGULATIONS CHECKLIST

Analyze the fact situation according to the TAPP rule.

**Print Version:**

1. Locate the relevant rule or regulation by using:

    a. The Parallel Table of Authorities in the *C.F.R. Index and Finding Aids* volume;

    b. The Descriptive Word Method in the same volume;

    c. The Topic Method; or

    d. The Agency Method.

2. Read and analyze the rule or regulation.

3. Update the rule or regulation through:

    a. The monthly *C.F.R. List of Sections Affected* and

    b. The most recent daily *Federal Register* cumulative list of sections affected.

4. Find interpretive cases by:

    a. *Shepard's C.F.R. Citations* for federal court decisions;

    b. Federal agency publications for federal agency decisions; or

    c. Unofficial reporters for both agency and federal court decisions, typically through loose leaf services.

5. Update the judicial opinion in the appropriate *Shepard's*.

**Electronic Version:**

1. Locate the relevant rule or regulation by using the methods described above through Lexis Advance or WestlawNext.

2. Both services continually update the regulation current within a few days.

3. Lexis Advance and WestlawNext provide citing references to interpretive cases.

4. Selected agency decisions are available through Lexis Advance or WestlawNext agency looseleaf libraries.

5.  Update all judicial opinions through *Shepard's* on Lexis Advance or KeyCite on WestlawNext.

**Internet Version:**

1.  Locate the relevant rule or regulation through the Parallel Table of Authorities or other methods described above using the FDsys e-CFR. Casemaker and Fastcase also provide access to the *C.F.R.*

2.  The e-CFR updates regulations within a couple of days.

3.  Locate interpretive agency opinions through the relevant agency websites or consult Casemaker or Fastcase coverage for selected agency opinions.

## E.  ADDITIONAL TIPS

1.  Locate the Patent and Trademark office website through usgovernmentmanual.gov or usa.gov/Agencies.shtml, for information on the overall process for submitting a trademark application, deadlines, and initial application forms.

2.  Note also the links at the website to the applicable federal statute, relevant *C.F.R.* provisions, and proposed and final rules.

3.  If the research process involves interpretive decisions from federal courts, electronic search services such as Lexis Advance and WestlawNext allow access to court documents, including district court filings, as well as appellate court briefs for all parties.

4.  Search the judges' names for information regarding their approaches to prior decisions involving trademark disputes.

5.  Similar links to attorneys' names provide information about their backgrounds and law firms.

6.  Secondary sources, such as law review, *A.L.R.*, or encyclopedia articles help understand basic concepts about areas of law, along with citations to further sources.

# Chapter 6

# STATE CONSTITUTIONAL LAW RESEARCH

## A. STATE CONSTITUTIONAL ORGANIZATION

Each state has its own constitution which is generally patterned after the United States Constitution. However, the length or scope of these state constitutions will vary. Some, like the federal Constitution, are relatively brief while others are so voluminous that they include materials which probably should be contained in statutes.

The number of constitutional amendments will also vary. The state constitutions have been amended more frequently than the federal Constitution. Generally, these changes occur at a significant time in the state's history. For example, several revisions of the Texas Constitution coincided with critical periods in the state's political history. Some examples include:

(1) 1836: The new republic adopted a constitution which bore a strong resemblance to the U.S. Constitution in its separation of powers provision and its bill of rights.

(2) 1845: Introduced the change from the status of a republic to that of a state.

(3) 1861: Effected the withdrawal from the Union and a change to the Confederacy.

(4) 1869: Effected the readmittance to the Union.

(5) 1876: The present Constitution. It is long and verbose and has been subject to many amendments.

It is important for the researcher to determine if there is a constitutional provision on point. This is particularly significant when a legislative issue is involved because the constitution gives the legislature power to act. As indicated in the discussion of the federal Constitution, legislative material is based on a hierarchy of law. The constitution is the highest authority of the state and becomes the first tier of legislative materials. State constitutions also enumerate certain powers to the state legislatures. These powers enable the legislatures to act by passing statutes. This form of legislation is the second tier of authority. In addition, the state legislatures have authority to create state administrative agencies which fashion the day-to-day rules and regulations to implement the statutes. These administrative rules and regulations become the third tier of authority.

> **HIERARCHY OF AUTHORITY**
> Constitution
> ↓
> State Statutes
> ↓
> State Administrative Rules and Regulations

The forms of publication are also similar to federal materials. In other words, there may be an official and unofficial publication of the constitution. At the present time, there are five states which have an official publication. These editions are printed by the State Legislative Council and may be the sole publication of the material within the state. However, the format and the research process for both the official and unofficial publication of a state constitution is basically the same. Once the researcher is familiar with the process, it is simply a matter of looking for that information to complete the research. For example, even the official publication of the code is annotated so that a case can be found. However, in two states, Nevada and Oregon, the annotations are not with the statutory provision but instead are found in separate binders.

As with other types of research, judicial interpretation of the state constitution is important. The annotated code is the most efficient way to find case authority for the constitutional material. However, alternate methods of both finding cases and updating the information are available. For example, the researcher can use the state digest under the appropriate topic and key number. In addition, the state edition of *Shepard's*, statutes volumes, provides not only updating information about the constitutional provision but also any cases that have interpreted the section.

Another source of information is local secondary authority. For instance, state encyclopedias frequently contain historical information or references to such available materials. In addition, local treatises or law journal articles written by practitioners, the state bar, or student authors may provide background information.

## B.  STATE CONSTITUTIONAL LAW LOCATION METHODS

### [1]  State Code Method

Finding the text of the state constitution is a relatively easy matter. Each of the state statutory codes has the text of that state's constitution; this format is similar to federal research in the *U.S.C.A.* or the *U.S.C.S.* for the United States Constitution. Generally, the constitutional volumes precede the statutory volumes. For example, in Texas, the first four volumes of the *Vernon's Annotated Texas Code* contain the Texas Constitution.

In addition, both an official and unofficial state code will be annotated. This is important because of the impact of judicial decisions on constitutional law. Case law has two important functions. First, judicial opinions provide the necessary interpretation to constitutional provisions which by necessity have to be general in nature. Second, the case law analyzes and reviews the statutory language or acts of the parties to determine if they meet the template outlined in the constitution.

The format for research materials is generally the same. Slight variations may exist because of the differences between the many publishers of the state codes. However, these minor differences should not be a problem for the researcher. The constitutional provision will be divided according to articles. Following this major heading, a number of research aids are noted such as: (1) a "table of contents" of the sections within that article; (2) any notations about the article itself such as its title or if it has been amended or repealed; (3) a table of revised section numbers for each revision; (4) the text of the first section; (5) legislative changes to that section; (6) historical notes about the section; (7) a list of law journal articles about that section; (8) an index to the notes of decisions; and (9) the listing of the cases.

## [2]  General Resources

Although the state code is the most commonly used method of finding a constitutional provision, there are other research tools available. The most notable is a multi-volume looseleaf set entitled *Constitutions of the United States: National and State* by Oceana Publications which contains the texts of the constitutions for all of the states. Because it uses a looseleaf format, it is kept current by frequent supplements. In 1980, a new and improved looseleaf index, arranged according to subject matter, was introduced entitled "Fundamental Liberties and Rights: A Fifty-State Index." In 1982, a second index entitled the "Laws, Legislature, Legislative Procedure: A Fifty-State Index" was added. As a companion text, the publisher has produced a *Digest of State Constitutions* which lists the subjects of constitutional provisions of the states in alphabetical order.

In addition, some states print pamphlets of the text. Due to lack of availability and the relatively small number of research aids that they contain, these are the least helpful resource tool.

## [3]  Historical Sources

Some legal research projects may require reviewing the provisions of prior constitutions or constitutional sections. As with current provisions, the best source of information is the state code.

Information from the constitutional conventions or drafters of the provision may prove to be a valuable research tool. Some state codes contain historical introductions to the constitution. In addition, the records, journals, proceedings, and other documents that may have been produced during the constitutional convention can be helpful.

---

### LOOKING FOR A STATE CONSTITUTIONAL PROVISION?

Does the subject matter raise a constitutional issue; is there a statute that implements the Constitution; or is the authority of the administrative agency questioned? If so, use one of the following methods:

1. Print Version:

    a. Descriptive Word Method: Use the key words and phrases in the General Index of the constitutional volumes.

    b. Topic Method: Go to the volume on that subject and then use the specific Individual Subject Index.

    c. Cross References: In most state codes, there are cross references that lead the researcher to the constitutional provision.

2. Electronic Version: the constitutional provision can be found on Lexis Advance or WestlawNext.

3. Internet Version: there are many websites that have a copy of the state constitutional provision or a link to where it can be found. For example, it can be found through the Texas Legislature website at http://www.constitution.legis.state.tx.us/.

Do you have a case that interprets a constitutional provision and you want more cases on this point? If so, locate as follows:

1. Print Version:

    a. Go to the constitutional provision and look under the Index of Notes of Decision to find the most appropriate note. Then check the bound volumes, pocket parts, and pamphlet supplements, if any.

    b. From the "one good case," obtain the topic and key number and use it in the various state digests.

2. Electronic Version: additional cases and resources can be found on Lexis Advance or WestlawNext. The researcher could find other similar cases through a digest method or secondary resources such as *A.L.R.*, treatises, law journal articles.

3. Internet Version: generally it is more difficult to find interpretive cases on an Internet website. But other secondary resources may be available.

---

The following example illustrates the process of locating information that relates to state constitutional law. The problem is one which raises a constitutional issue.

**EXAMPLE #1:** John Miller attends public school. The school district has a regulation that restricts the length that male students can wear their hair. John knows about the regulation but refuses to cut his hair. On January 15, 2014, John was suspended from school for violating this regulation. He complains that this regulation violates the equal rights amendment to the Texas Constitution because it only applies to male students. Is the regulation unconstitutional under the equal rights amendment?

1. *The Topic Method.* If the researcher has some familiarity with constitutional law, it will be apparent that this is an equal rights problem. Therefore, by using the Topic Method, the researcher will go to the Index for the constitutional volumes which is located in volume one after the unannotated copy of the Texas Constitution and look for the subsection of "equality." The Index will refer the researcher to "Generally, Art. 1, § 3." However, the more specific equal rights amendment follows the general provision and is noted as § 3a, "equality under the law." The researcher could also look in the General Index.

2. *The Descriptive Word Method.* The researcher could also use the Descriptive Word Method to solve this problem. This method should be used if the researcher is not as familiar with the topic area, and thus, a more thorough analysis of the problem is necessary. The first step in the research process would be to analyze the facts. Using the TAPP rule, the following analysis might be used:

| | |
|---|---|
| Things: | hair, hair length policy |
| Acts: | discrimination, suspension, equality, equal rights |
| Persons: | students, public schools, schools |
| Places: | campus |

## C.  FINDING AND UPDATING A CONSTITUTIONAL PROVISION

### [1]  Print Version

1. *Index Bound Volume:* Use the key words and phrases in either the Index for the constitutional volumes or the General Index if it is more detailed. The key words for this problem are: sex discrimination and equal rights. These words would lead the researcher to Art. 1, § 3 and § 3a of the Texas Constitution.

2. *Index Pocket Part:* The index information as well as all other materials must be updated in the pocket part. The updated index of the Index for the Constitution volumes is located before the updated annotated text of the constitution in the pocket part. The General Index is published every two years in a softbound cover, and therefore, it has no pocket part.

3. *Read and Analyze the Provision in the Bound Volume:* The researcher must read carefully the constitutional provision in the bound volume. As the researcher will find, it is only a very general provision and does not specifically answer the question. It merely indicates that "equality under the law shall not be denied or abridged because of sex, race, color, creed, or national origin." Part of the analysis process is to review the research aids to determine if there is any other relevant information. For example, there are historical notes which indicate when the amendment

became law, cross references to related statutory materials, a list of law journal articles on related subjects, library references to topic and key numbers in the digests, and related federal statutes and cases. These research aids should be scanned to see if there are any appropriate research tools.

4.  *Pocket Part:* Update the constitutional provision. This should be done by reviewing the pocket part in the back of the volume. In this problem, there are no changes or additions to the provision.

5.  *Supplementary Pamphlet:* If any pamphlet supplements have been published on an interim basis, these pamphlets should be checked.

6.  *Update the Provision:* The final update would be to update the provision in *Shepard's Texas Citations*, statutes volume. This step would indicate if the provision has been amended or repealed. The researcher can update the provision through *Shepard's* in print or on Lexis Advance or KeyCite through WestlawNext.

## [2]  Electronic Version

The researcher can also do state constitutional research electronically. Both Lexis Advance and WestlawNext have the state constitutions available through the state statutory databases. For example, the researcher could find the relevant constitutional provision for Example #1 by using the terms "Texas Constitution equality." Both Tex. Const. art. I, § 3 and Tex. Const. art. I, § 3a will be found.

## [3]  Internet Version

There are many websites that have a copy of the state constitutional provision or a link to where it can be found. For example, it can be found through the Texas Legislature website at http://www.constitution.legis.state.tx.us/.

## D.  FINDING AND UPDATING INTERPRETIVE CASES

Once the researcher has located and updated the constitutional provision, it is important to find interpretive cases. Typically, the constitutional provision is general and vague, and therefore will not answer the researcher's specific question. Thus, interpretive cases or statutes will help the researcher answer the question. The following methods show you how to answer the legal question asked in the previous example by searching for judicial interpretation of the constitutional provision:

## [1]  Print Version

1.  *Bound Volume:* Following the research aids is an Index for the Notes of Decision. Again, use the key words and phrases from the TAPP rule analysis. There is a subheading under "sex discrimination" for schools which leads to Note of Decision number 19. Under this note, there are two relevant cases: *Mercer v. Board of Trustees, North Forest ISD,* 538 S.W.2d 201 (Tex. Civ. App — Houston [14th Dist.] 1976) and *Toungate v.*

*Board of Trustees of Bastrop ISD*, 842 S.W.2d 823 (Tex. App. — Austin 1992). The researcher would find that the *Toungate* case was reversed and rendered in 958 S.W.2d 365 (Tex. 1997).

2. *Pocket Part:* The interpretive cases must also be updated. This should be done through the pocket part in the back of the volume by checking Note of Decision number 19.

3. *Pamphlet Supplement:* Any pamphlet supplements that are available should be checked.

4. *Update:* The actual opinions of the cases that will be used in a legal memorandum or appellate brief should be read and analyzed. Then they should be Shepardized in *Shepard's Texas Citations*, case volume, if they are Texas cases and the researcher is using the print volumes or *Shepard's* on Lexis Advance or KeyCite on WestlawNext.

Traditionally in Texas, there is also another step in updating cases. The *Subsequent History Table* must be consulted to see if either the Texas Supreme Court (the court of last resort for civil cases) or the Texas Court of Criminal Appeals (the court of last resort for criminal cases) has agreed to review the case. There are three volumes that must be checked. They are: the green paper bound volume of the *Texas Subsequent History Table* (contains information for the last year); the advance sheets of the *Southwestern Reporter, Third Series; Texas Cases* (contain information within the last six weeks); and the *Texas Supreme Court Journal* (contains weekly information). Effective 2014, West has decided not to publish the annual *Texas Subsequent History Table*. The advance sheets of the *Southwestern Reporter, Third Series; Texas Cases*, however, will continue to be published as will the *Texas Supreme Court Journal* and those sources need to be checked if the researcher is using the print version.

## [2]  Electronic Version

A potential problem is that the *Toungate* case which was found through print research was not found through the case note heading of "Constitutional Law: Equal Protection: Gender & Sex" under either § 3 or § 3a. This is potentially a problem if the researcher ends the research at this point. If none specifically talk about haircut cases, Shepardize the section.

At the top right of Tex. Const. Art. I, Section 3a, there is a *Shepard's* box. Click Shepardize this document inside the box and the researcher will be provided with two options. The whole section of the provision can be Shepardize or just subsection 3a. Generally, using the more specific section is preferable. If the whole section is selected, the researcher gets 264 citing cases. But this is too many and not all on the specific issue of haircuts. Therefore, use the Search Within Results filter at the bottom left side of the page and type in haircut.

After searching for haircut, the researcher gets six cases — one federal case and five state cases. The very first case listed is the Texas Supreme Court decision in *Toungate*. It reverses *Toungate v. Board of Trustees of Bastrop ISD*, 842 S.W.2d 823 (Tex. App. — Austin 1992). This lower court decision is also in the list. By

Shepardizing and searching this way, the researcher now has a total of six potential cases.

In addition, any cases that were found would need to be updated through *Shepard's* on Lexis Advance or KeyCite on WestlawNext. This update method would give you the full subsequent history in one step.

## [3]  Internet Version

There are many places to find state constitutions. For example, Texas.gov has a copy of the Texas Constitution and statutes at http://www.texas.gov/en/search/Pages/results.aspx?q=Texas%20Constitution. In addition, the Texas Constitution can be found at www.capitol.state.tx.us/.

For a listing of state resources, see LexisNexis InfoPro hosts Zimmerman's Research Guides. For a listing of Texas resources, see http://law.lexisnexis.com/infopro/zimmermans/disp.aspx?z=2001.

Generally it is more difficult to find interpretive cases on an Internet website. But other secondary resources may be available.

**EXAMPLE #2:** The researcher is aware that there is a federal Defense of Marriage Act (DOMA) but that there are also state constitutional or statutory provisions defining marriage as between one man and one woman. The researcher wants to know if there is a Texas state constitutional provision on the subject.

Using the Descriptive Word Method, the researcher could use the word "constitution" and the subheading of "marriage, gender" in the Descriptive Word Index. This would lead the researcher to Article 1, § 32 of the Texas Constitution. This constitutional provision states that "Marriage in this state shall consist only of the union of one man and one woman."

By using the word "marriage" and the subheading of "same sex, prohibition," the researcher would be led to Family Code § 2.001. This provision states that a marriage license can only be issued to a man and a woman desiring to marry and cannot be issued to persons of the same sex. In the pocket part, the research references and cases are listed. Obviously, the constitutional provision is the most relevant provision.

The same process as described in the previous example should be used for updating the constitutional provision and finding and updating a relevant case. In the bound volume, there are no amendments, but there is one interpretive case and some library references. In the pocket part, there is another recent case, *Leon v. Perry*, 975 F. Supp. 2d 632 (W.D. Tex. 2014). It concerns various issues such as the validity of the provision which would be critical information. This underscores the necessity to always check the pocket part.

In addition, there are research references to secondary sources such as *A.L.R.*, encyclopedias, form books, and treatises. For example, there is a reference to the state encyclopedia, *Tex. Jur. 3d*, under Family Law § 316 which leads to Texas Family Code § 6.204(b). The code provision states that "A marriage between persons of the same sex or a civil union is contrary to the public policy of this state and is void in this state." That section also referenced a Comment in a law journal on DOMA — Comment, *A Prediction of the United States Supreme Court's Analysis of the Defense of Marriage Act, After* Lawrence v. Texas, 46 S. TEX. L. REV. 361 (2004).

The pocket part listed the *Leon v. Perry* case and also several other cases including *J.B. and H.B.*, 326 S.W.3d 654 (Tex. App. — Dallas 2010) and *State v. Naylor*, 330 S.W.3d 434 (Tex. App. — Austin 2011). The Texas Supreme Court granted the petition for review in both of these cases in 2013. Therefore, the researcher would need to follow the case to determine the disposition by the Texas Supreme Court. This could be done through the print version of the *Texas Supreme Court Journal* or through *Shepard's* on Lexis Advance or KeyCite on WestlawNext.

> **EXAMPLE #3:** The senior partner asks a follow-up question. If Texas does not recognize same sex marriage, do Texas courts have subject matter jurisdiction to adjudicate a divorce petition of a same-sex marriage even if a marriage was entered in another state that recognizes the validity of same-sex marriages?

This may be the situation where the researcher starts with secondary authority to find a case. The Index for *Tex. Jur.* 3d has a heading for same-sex couples and a subsection for annulment which leads to Family Law § 316 and divorce which leads to Family Law § 413. Both sections have the *J.B.* and *Naylor* cases. Both sections also cite to Texas Family Code § 6.204.

> **EXAMPLE #4:** The senior partner heard that an Austin woman filed a federal lawsuit seeking to stop the Social Security Administration's practice of withholding spousal benefits from couples who live in states, like Texas, with laws banning same-sex marriage. The senior partner wants the researcher to find the story and to track its progress through the courts.

To find the story, the researcher could do a Google search. This would lead to the Austin American Statesman newspaper website at statesman.com where the story could be found. To find the court filings and track the case, the researcher could use PACER or Bloomberg. Once the case is at the appellate level, the researcher could use either Lexis Advance or WestlawNext to find the case and court documents.

## STATE CONSTITUTIONAL CHECKLIST

**Print Version:**

1.  Analyze the facts to determine the key words and phrases using:

    a.  The Topic Method; or

    b.  The Descriptive Word Method.

2.  Use the key words and phrases in the Index to the constitutional volumes of *Vernon's Annotated Texas Statutes (VATS)* or the General Index.

3.  Read the relevant constitutional provision.

4.  Review the research aids that follow the relevant section.

5.  Update the constitutional provision by:

    a.  The pocket part in the back of the bound volume;

    b.  Any pamphlet supplement; and

    c.  *Shepard's Texas Citations*, statutes volume. The researcher can update the provision through Shepard's in print or on Lexis Advance or KeyCite through WestlawNext.

6.  Find appropriate interpretive cases, if any, by:

    a.  Looking at the Index of Decisions for a specific Note of Decision; and

    b.  Finding a pertinent Note of Decision number in the bound volumes, pocket parts, and possible pamphlet supplements.

7.  Update the case law by:

    a.  The pocket part in the back of the bound volume;

    b.  Any pamphlet supplement;

    c.  Reading and analyzing cases;

    d.  *Shepard's Texas Citations*, case volume, or on Lexis Advance or KeyCite on WestlawNext; and

    e.  Subsequent History. If there is subsequent history, then it must be cited. If the researcher were using an electronic version, the process would be simple by using *Shepard's* on Lexis Advance or KeyCite on WestlawNext as that information would be available in one easy step. In Texas and some other states, there are subsequent history tables in print version. To find the subsequent history in Texas, there has traditionally been an annual paper bound volume, cumulative table in the advance sheets of the *Southwestern Reporter, Third Series, Texas Cases*, and the *Texas Supreme Court Journal.*

**Electronic Version:**

1.  Find the appropriate constitutional provision through either a topic or descriptive word approach.

2. Analyze the provision.

3. Review the research aids to determine if there are other primary or secondary authorities.

4. Use the case notes following the provision on Lexis Advance or WestlawNext.

5. Read the case in the appropriate reporter.

6. Update the case through *Shepard's* on Lexis Advance or KeyCite on WestlawNext.

**Internet Version:**

1. There are many websites that have a copy of the state constitutional provision or a link to where it can be found.

2. Check the state legislature's website where the constitution usually can be found.

## E.   ADDITIONAL TIPS

1. LexisNexis InfoPro hosts Zimmerman's Research Guides. For a listing of Texas resources, see http://law.lexisnexis.com/infopro/zimmermans/disp. aspx?z=2001.

2. Texas Jurisprudence, an encyclopedia which was discussed in this chapter, can be searched on both Lexis Advance and WestlawNext.

3. There are many places to find state constitutions in both print and electronic versions. For example, Texas.gov has a copy of the Texas Constitution and statutes at http://www.texas.gov/en/search/Pages/results.aspx?q=Texas%20Constitution or the Texas Constitution can be found at www.capitol.state.tx.us/.

4. FindLaw has state materials. For example, Texas materials can be found at http://www.findlaw.com/casecode/texas.html.

5. Through the Legislative Reference Library of Texas, the researcher can find a wealth of information covering the Texas Constitution, amendments, statutory information, and legislative history. The Texas Legislative Council has all of the amendments to the constitution since 1876. Knowing the historical development of the law can be very helpful.

6. Other sources are available such as Oceana Publications' looseleaf service entitled *Constitutions of the United States: National and State* which contains the texts of the constitutions for all of the states. As a companion text, the publisher has produced a *Digest of State Constitutions* which lists the subjects of constitutional provisions of the states in alphabetical order.

7. Carolina Academic Press has a series entitled Legal Research Series which has legal research books that are state specific for 27 states. They would lead the researcher to state constitutional research as well as other types of primary and secondary authority for those states.

# Chapter 7

# STATE LEGISLATIVE RESEARCH

## A.  STATE LAW ORGANIZATION

### [1]  Overview

Most new law students read many state judicial opinions and often research such opinions as their first exposure to the ways of finding legal sources. As a consequence, there is a tendency to see all legal problems as a quest for common law decisions. Most practitioners, however, confront daily problems involving state statutes. Thus, finding these statutes and checking for any amendments becomes a routine task.

Because statutory language is often ambiguous, it is necessary to clarify its meaning. For example, to determine the purpose or intent of the legislature, the researcher would need to examine the legislative history of the act. Case law or State Attorney General Opinions that interpret the statute or its language would also be relevant. Finally, the rules or decisions by administrative agencies or boards might help the researcher to interpret the law as well. Thus, it is important for the researcher to recognize that legal research is an integrated process that requires different levels and types of research.

In addition, a statute in one state may be based on a similar federal or sister state statute. For example, the Civil Rights Act of 1964 has been a template for many state statutes with only minor variances. Many states have adopted uniform laws prepared by the National Conference on Uniform State Laws. Therefore, if an act has a provision that is identical to a provision in another jurisdiction, interpretive case law from the sister jurisdiction may be persuasive authority.

### [2]  Pattern of Publication

State statutory materials are published in the same pattern of publication as the federal statutory materials. Thus, a law is first published in the form of a slip law. At the end of the legislative session, the more commonly used session laws are published. The final form of publishing laws is in the codes and annotated codes. The following chart demonstrates the particular characteristics of each stage of publication. General statements are made about the publications and a specific state example is used.

| STAGES OF PUBLICATION | | |
|---|---|---|
| **Form** | **Generally** | **Specifically — Texas** |
| Slip Laws | 1. Issued in most states.<br>2. Rarely used by the public. | 1. No official publication. |
| Session Laws | 1. Each state publishes a set that is similar to the Statutes at Large.<br><br><br><br><br>2. They are the authoritative text.<br>3. Generally, there are long delays in printing.<br><br><br>4. Non-cumulative indices. | 1. Published on a regular basis under both the republic and State of Texas, *i.e.*, since 1941. West publishes the *General and Special Laws — Texas* in two volumes for every legislative session.<br>2. Same.<br><br>3. Same. However, there are unofficial advance services. For example, *Vernon's Texas Session Law Service* (West).<br>4. Same. |
| Codes | 1. Format is similar to the *U.S.C.*<br>2. Subject access.<br>3. Commercially published.<br>4. Generally unofficial.<br>5. Generally annotated.<br>6. Authority varies.<br>7. Supplemented — generally on an annual basis. | 1. Same. Vernon Annotated Texas Statutes.<br>2. Same.<br>3. Published by West.<br>4. Quasi-official.<br>5. Annotated.<br>6. Not authoritative.<br>7. Annual pocket parts and semi-annual pamphlets. |

Electronic access to statutes is available at official state websites; for example, Texas statutes appear at the Texas legislature's webpage (tlc.state.tx.us). Lexis Advance and WestlawNext contain all current state annotated codes. Fastcase and Casemaker also provide access to all current state codes.

## B. STATE LAW LOCATION METHODS

Before the research process begins, you should examine the code to see how it is organized. For national access to state resources, a good starting point might be the Library of Congress State Government Information page links to the homepage for each state (www.loc.gov/rr/news/stategov/stategov.html). An alternative website is whpgs.org/f.htm, which provides links to all 50 states' statutory and administrative codes, bills, and city ordinances. The initial screen indicates currentcy of material and can run several months behind official and unofficial sources. After reviewing how the state materials are organized, the typical researcher should proceed to the annotated state code, where statutory language, legislative history references, and interpretive cases appear in one source. Depending on your familiarity with the code, the subject matter, and the information available, you can use the popular name approach, topic method, or the descriptive word method to find the relevant provision.

---

**LOOKING FOR A STATE STATUTE?**

Do you have the popular name of the statute? If so, use the following methods:

1.  Use the *Popular Name Table* in the state annotated code, if one exists.

2.  If one does not exist in the state code, then check *Shepard's Acts and Cases by Popular Names*, online or in the hardcopy general index.

If you do not have the popular name of the statute, or if the statute does not have a popular name, use one of the following methods:

3.  Topic Method: If familiar with the code, go directly to the relevant title. Once in the appropriate title, scan the outline in front of the title to find the relevant chapter and section or consult the individual title's index, typically located in the last volume of the title.

4.  Descriptive Word Method: Use the key words and phrases from the TAPP rule analysis in the General Index.

---

The following example will demonstrate how a problem can be researched. Although this is a Texas problem, the research techniques can be used in any state code. The names of the publications may be slightly different; however, they will generally contain the same types of research materials.

**EXAMPLE #1:** A Texas police officer has pulled over a motorist driving a new vehicle. Even though there is a chrome decorative plate holder, the license plate itself is displayed in the front windshield. The driver received a citation for running a stop sign and a misdemeanor violation of a state law requiring proper display of a license place.

## [1]  Popular Name Method

Unlike federal statutory sources, an annotated state code may not have a popular name table. Texas, however, has a popular name table in the paperbound *General Index* to the annotated state code, as does WestlawNext. In addition, *Shepard's Acts and Cases by Popular Names* on Lexis Advance or in print lists both federal and state statutes by name; therefore, if there is a popular name, consult a popular name table.

## [2]  Topic Method

Each print code has an Individual Subject Index, often in the last volume of that subject. Thus, for example, the *Probate Code* has its own index and the *Property Code* has its individual index. If the researcher has a good working knowledge of the code and the subject matter, it is possible to make "an educated guess" as to where the statutory material will be located. It is then a matter of determining the key words and phrases for the problem, and then using those words in the volume containing the *Individual Subject Index* and its pocket part supplement. The example above would work well with the topic method if the researcher identified the problem as part of the "Transportation Code."

## [3] Descriptive Word Method

It is more likely that the researcher will have to use the descriptive word method. Therefore, the process should begin with analysis of the facts according to the TAPP rule. Then these key words and phrases would be used in the *General Index* for the state code or as a word search on Lexis Advance or WestlawNext. Be sure to choose your state's jurisdiction in the search box.

The first step for solving this problem is to analyze the facts according to the TAPP rule. Some words that might be used in this analysis are:

| | |
|---|---|
| Things: | motor vehicle, license plate |
| Acts: | display of plates, crimes and offenses |
| Persons: | driver |
| Places: | N/A |

## C. FINDING AND UPDATING A STATE STATUTE

### [1] Print Version

1. *Index Volume:* Use the key words for the problem in *Vernon's Annotated Texas Statutes General Index.* In this problem, the key words are "motor vehicles" and "crimes and offenses," leading to the Transportation Code § 502.473 *et seq.* pertaining to proper display of license plates. Although the *VATS* index is paperbound, be sure to check the pocket part of any hard cover index.

2. *Read and Analyze the Provision in the Bound Volume:* Once found, the statute should be read and analyzed. Part of the analysis is to review the research aids that follow the relevant section. However, in most cases, language regarding the effective date of the legislation should be checked to make sure that this act was in effect at the time that the problem arose. Furthermore, legislative history could be important depending on the particular problem and the information that is needed. A later section of this chapter discusses legislative history in more detail.

3. *Pocket Part:* Update the statutory provision in the annual pocket part in the back of the bound volume under the title and section number of the statute.

4. *Supplementary Pamphlet:* Depending on the amount of material that is available since the pocket part was issued, there might be a semi-annual pamphlet supplement. If one exists, then it should also be consulted by looking under the title and section number of the statute.

5. *Session Law Service:* Statutes are also updated by a session law service on a regular basis when the legislature is in session. Thus, the latest issue of *Vernon's Texas Session Law Service* should be checked.

6. *Update the Provision:* Finally, *Shepard's* state citations or statutes volumes should also be used to indicate whether the statute has been repealed or amended.

## [2]  Electronic Version

1. Locate the provision on Lexis Advance or WestlawNext, using the same words or phrases noted above.

2. Note the statute's currency as indicated by Lexis Advance or WestlawNext. Because both services update laws continuously, there is no need to check the print session law services.

3. Update the provision with *Shepard's* on Lexis Advance or KeyCite on WestlawNext.

## [3]  Internet Version

Locate the provision through an official state website, such as the Texas Legislature Online (tlc.state.tx.us). There are no interpretive decisions, though the laws are current through the last legislative session. Fastcase and Casemaker provide coverage of all 50 state codes continuously updated.

## D.  FINDING AND UPDATING INTERPRETIVE CASES

The next step in the research process is to find interpretive case law. These cases will interpret specific statutory language, as well as determine whether a provision is either constitutional or valid. The method for finding interpretive case law is as follows:

## [1]  Print Version

1. *Bound Volume:* In print, use the key words and phrases in the Index to the Notes of Decisions directly following the statutory language to find the most appropriate Note for relevant cases, if any. In V.A.T.S., the relevant Note is "Display of License Plates, Note 11 following § 502.473. The Texas court of last resort for criminal appeals ruled that license plate placement on a dashboard did not comply with the statutory requirement of the "front" of the vehicle.

2. *Pocket Part:* Check the annual pocket part supplement in the back of the bound volume for additional cases, if any.

3. *Pamphlet Supplement:* In Texas, pamphlet supplements are issued on a semi-annual basis.

4. *Advance Sheets:* More current case updates can be checked in the advance sheets of the regional reporter, e.g., *Southwestern Reporter, Third Series*, Texas Cases. These advance sheets contain a section

entitled "Statutes Construed" Table. This table lists the recent cases that have interpreted statutory provisions. Lexis Advance and WestlawNext provide ongoing access to recent decisions, eliminating the need for steps two through four.

5. *Update: Shepard's Texas Citations*, case volumes, should be used to verify and update the status of the case. Again, Lexis Advance provides access to *Shepard's* and WestlawNext updates through KeyCite.

## [2] Electronic Version

1. Check Notes of Decisions located with the statute through Lexis Advance or WestlawNext. These services provide ongoing access to recent decisions, eliminating the need for steps two through four above.

2. Update the relevant cases with *Shepard's* on Lexis Advance or KeyCite on WestlawNext.

## [3] Internet Version

Official state legislative websites provide no access to interpretive decisions. Fastcase and Casemaker provide interpretive decisions for some jurisdictions. Casemaker's Statute Annotator shows how courts have interpreted or cited statutes.

---

### STATE STATUTORY CHECKLIST

Analyze the facts according to the TAPP rule.

**Print Version:**

1. Find the appropriate statute by:

    a. Popular Name in:

        (1) The *Popular Name Table*, if it exists, in the state code index; or

        (2) *Shepard's Acts and Cases by Popular Names* in print;

    b. Topic Method: Use the Individual Subject Index;

    c. Descriptive Word Method: Use the *General* Index.

2. Read the relevant statutory provision in the bound volume.

3. Review the research aids that follow the relevant section.

4. Update the statutory provision by:

    a. The annual pocket part supplement;

    b. Any pamphlet supplements (semi-annual);

    c. A session law service; and

    d. Update with *Shepard's Citations*, statutes volumes, for relevant jurisdiction.

5. Find interpretive case law by:

---

     a. The Index to the Notes of Decision immediately following the statute's language; and

     b. The appropriate Note of Decision number in the bound volume.

6. Update the case law by:

     a. The annual pocket part supplement;

     b. Any semi-annual pamphlet supplements;

     c. Advance sheets of the regional reporter, state cases volumes, *Statutes Construed Table*.

     d. Update relevant decisions with *Shepard's* specific state *Citations*.

## Electronic Version:

1. Find the appropriate statute by:

     a. Popular Name in:

        (1) The *Popular Name Table* on the Lexis Advance or WestlawNext versions of the state code index; or

        (2) *Shepard's Acts and Cases by Popular Names* through Lexis Advance.

     b. Topic Method: Individual Subject Index through Lexis Advance or WestlawNext.

     c. Descriptive Word Method: Use the *General* Index through Lexis Advance or WestlawNext.

2. Read the relevant provision.

3. Review the research aids following the provision.

4. Update the statute by checking the currency designation.

5. Find current cases Notes of Decision following the statute.

6. Update the cases through *Shepard's* on Lexis Advance or KeyCite on WestlawNext.

## Internet Version:

Access to official state websites provides current statutes with update notices. For example, Texas statutes are available at the Texas Legislature Council website, tlc.state.tx.us. There are no interpretive decisions or other references at this official site. Fastcase and Casemaker offer access to Texas statutes, as well as those from all other states. Interpretive decisions are available for some states. Casemaker's Statute Annotator shows how courts have interpreted or cited statutes.

## E. STATE LEGISLATIVE HISTORY

### [1] Overview

The purpose of locating state legislative history is the same as that at the federal level — to determine the legislature's intent or to analyze any language changes in the statute. These legislative histories also include the same types of material as those at the federal level, such as committee reports, copies of the proposed bills and any amendments, committee hearings, and floor debates.

Finding legislative history at the federal level is a relatively easy matter compared to locating state legislative history, because what is available will vary greatly between the states. Generally, the legislatures will not publish their debates, committee reports, or hearings. Sometimes, a state legislature will tape this information and a transcript of the tape can be obtained. In Texas, the most accessible official documents are the Senate and House Journals. However, the problem with these research tools is that the Journals only contain brief minutes of the proceedings and the final vote on the legislation. Individual state websites are good starting points. USA.gov has a state government page with links to the official websites of every state, as does the Library of Congress state government information page referenced earlier in this chapter.

### [2] Locating Legislative History

Finding state legislative history can be a problem. The first source the researcher should check is the annotated state code. Under the research aids, it is possible to get some idea as to any documents that might exist, including the bill numbers. This information allows access to various legislative history components. Another alternative is a specific state's legislative information website; for example, *The Guide to Texas Legislative Information* website (tlc.state.tx.us) includes links to the Texas Legislature Online (TLO) and the Legislative Reference Library. Lexis Advance and WestlawNext offer some state legislative history, but generally the researcher will find more comprehensive materials with state government materials.

> **EXAMPLE #2:** The Texas Court of Criminal Appeals decision located earlier in this chapter references 1991 amendments to the disputed statute. Find the Bill Analysis for the Texas legislation proposed in the 1991 session to amend the law of vehicle registration insignia.
>
> 1. Consult the annotated Texas statute addressing the issue and check the "Historical and Statutory Notes" for enactments in 1991. This will indicate a chapter and section number for the law: the 72d legislature, ch. 765.
>
> 2. Because the law was enacted after 1973, the Legislative Reference Library (lrl.state.tx.us) website will include each component of the legislative history, organized by bill number or chapter number, along with the legislative session number.
>
> 3. Using those numbers, locate the reports and read them to determine whether they address the location of license plates.

| LEGISLATIVE HISTORY CHECKLIST | | | |
|---|---|---|---|
| **Federal** | | **Texas** | |
| 1. | Discover what language interests you and when this language was added, amended, or repealed. | 1. | Same. |
| 2. | Determine what legislative history is available by: | 2. | Same and consult the state legislature's website providing links to available documents. E.g., The Guide to Texas Legislative Information website (tlc.state.tx.us). |
| a. | Checking the annotated code | | |
| b. | Using a commercial publication such as Johnson, *Sources of Compiled Legislative History Laws* | | |
| 3. | Go to the research finding tools such as: | 3. | Same. |
| a. | C.I.S. — since 1970 | a. | Legislative Reference Library website after 1973. |
| b. | *U.S.C.C.A.N.* — has only selected histories | b. | State Archives |
| c. | *CCH Congressional Index* | c. | House and Senate Journals — record daily activities |
| 4. | Find the appropriate sources of legislative history: | 4. | Same. |
| a. | Primary sources: | a. | Primary sources: Except for attorney general opinions, items below available at Legislative Reference Library website lrl.tx.state.us |
| | (1) Public law | | (1) Statutes |
| | (2) Bills and amendments | | (2) Original bill files for fiscal notes and analysis — before 1943 — print only at Texas State Library. |
| | (3) Committee reports | | (3) Committee minutes — begin at TLO website and coordinate to Legislative Reference Library website |

| | |
|---|---|
| (4) Debates | (4) Debates — no printed versions since 1973, audios through House/Senate media offices. Since 2001, floor debate videos available at TLO website |
| (5) Committee hearings | (5) Hearings — after 1973 available on audiotapes from House/Senate media offices |
| (6) Presidential Messages, etc. | (6) Governor's Messages |
| (7) Attorney General Opinions | (7) Attorney General Opinions — at texasattorneygeneral.gov |
| b.   Secondary sources: | b.   Secondary sources: |
| (1) Newspaper clippings | (1) Newspaper clippings — daily clipping service for media link |
| (2) Law review articles | (2) Law review articles |
| | (3) Legislative clipping service |
| | (4) "Accomplishments of the Legislature" |

## F.  MUNICIPAL LEGISLATION

### [1]  Municipal Law Organization

Local governments, such as cities and counties, are usually called municipal corporations. As a general rule, they obtain their power from the state. Thus, if the research problem involves a question of the city or county's authority to act, the state constitution or statutes must be examined.

There are two kinds of legislative materials that are available at the local level. The first is the charter of the municipal corporation. It is analogous to the state constitution. In larger cities, the municipal charter generally is published in the same volumes that contain the city code. However, in smaller cities, the form of publication may vary. In some cities there is no accessible, up-to-date compilation of legislative materials. Thus, city charters would have to be obtained from the city or county clerk's office. A growing number of cities, however, provide access to their charters through a home page.

The second type of legislation is an ordinance. Ordinances, analogous to state statutes, are enacted by the local governing body such as the city council. The publication of ordinances will also vary according to the size of the city. For example, they may be printed in the city code, an official journal of the governing body, in slip form, or in the local newspaper. Like city charters, municipal ordinances are now frequently available at a city's website.

Municipal codes have one major distinguishing characteristic: they are rarely annotated. This has a significant impact on the research method for finding interpretive case law. Because there are no cases readily available, alternative sources must be consulted.

## [2]   Municipal Law Location Methods

The most common method of researching a city charter or ordinance is through the city code. However, if an ordinance has not been codified, copies of it may be obtained through the city clerk's office. City codes are similar to the state codes in that they contain the text of the ordinance or charter, topical analysis, historical notes, cross references, indices, and tables of the location of earlier sections in the new code.

### [a]   Print Version

Municipal codes are usually published in looseleaf format. This has an impact on the research process because looseleaf services are updated by removing the outdated page and inserting the current page. Before an ordinance can be cited, it is important to confirm that the page that is in the binder is the most current page. To do this, the publisher generally has a designation at the bottom of the page which identifies the issuance of the material by date or number. This information must be compared with pages in the front of the binder which are generally called "checklists."

### [b]   Electronic Version

Lexis Advance and WestlawNext provide coverage of some municipal codes along with currency status.

### [c]   Internet Version

A number of municipalities provide Internet access through code publishing companies, such as Municipal Law Corporation (municode.com) and American Legal Publishing Corp. (amlegal.com). These sources indicate the most recent version of the Code in a manner simpler than that described below for print sources. Fastcase and Casemaker also offer some municipal codes in their state libraries.

## [3]   Finding and Updating Interpretive Cases

### [a]   Print Version

In print, the first source is the *state digest*. By analyzing the facts to find a case in the digest as discussed in Chapter 2, the researcher can find the appropriate topic and key number. The second source is a *treatise*. There are several sources in the area of municipal law which are updated on a regular basis. They are the current editions of E. McQuillin's *Law of Municipal Corporations*, a multi-volume set with annual index, and the Sandra M. Stephenson and Chester James Antieau's *Antieau on Local Government Law*, as well as *Ordinance Law Annotations*, published by West and updated annually. These volumes organize the material according to subject matter and list the relevant cases. The set also has a two-volume table of cases organized by state and county or city. Any relevant decisions should be Shepardized in appropriate state *Shepard's Citations*.

## [b]  Electronic Version

Lexis Advance and WestlawNext provide case citations, if any, to municipal codes. Secondary sources, such as *Antieau on Local Government Law*, through Lexis Advance, or *Ordinance Law Annotations* through WestlawNext, may provide some decisions. Update any relevant decisions through *Shepard's* on Lexis Advance of KeyCite on WestlawNext.

---

### LOOKING FOR A CITY ORDINANCE?

Are you looking for an answer to a local problem? If so, check:

1.  The city charter if it is like a constitutional issue; or

2.  The city ordinance if it is more like a statutory problem.

If a local problem exists, how do you find the local charter or ordinance?

3.  Use the topic method if you are familiar with the code;

4.  Use the descriptive word method in the code's general index section if you are not familiar with the organization of the material; or

5.  Use secondary sources such as a treatise if you need a general description of local law.

If you need to do a comparative study of municipal ordinances, how do you get the information?

6.  Use *Ordinance Law Annotations*; or

7.  Other secondary sources, such as one of the two major treatises on municipal corporations, *Law of Municipal Corporations* or *Antieau on Local Government Law*.

---

This problem is based on the San Antonio, Texas City Code. The research process will be similar for other city codes.

**EXAMPLE #3:** Does the city code require businesses to accommodate transgender individuals?

## [4]  Finding and Updating a City Ordinance

As with other legislative problems, the first step is to analyze the facts according to the TAPP rule. The key phrases in this situation are "public accommodation" or "transgender." The following process should be used.

## [a]   Print Version

1.   Index: Use the key words and phrases in the Index to the City Code or the City of San Antonio website link to the code under the "Your Government" tab. A caveat: the Code may have two indices — one for the city charter and the other for the ordinances. Be certain that you are in the proper index or else you will not find the information. The ordinance can be found in the "Administration" chapter.

2.   Read and Analyze the Provision: The researcher must read the relevant section.

3.   Update the Provision: The researcher must note the page number where the provision is found and the date or supplement number at the bottom of the page or in parentheses following the provision's language. This information is important in the updating process.

The next step is to turn to the checklist in the front of the volume or the website's notice of the last update. Sometimes there will be discrepancies in these numbers. However, if the number at the bottom of the page of the text is at least as large as the number on the checklist, then the information is current. In the present case, the information is current.

## [b]   Electronic Version

Lexis Advance and WestlawNext provide access to some city codes along with currency status.

## [c]   Electronic Version

Consult the city website for links to the city code or code publishing companies, such as Municipal Law Corporation (municode.com) or American Legal Publishing Corp. (amlegal.com). Fastcase and Casemaker have some city codes in their state libraries.

## [5]   Finding and Updating Interpretive Cases

The next step in the research process is to find interpretive case law, if any. This may be done in several ways. The most common methods are outlined below.

## [a]  Print Version

1.  Annotated Codes: Sometimes a municipal code will be annotated, but this is rare.

2.  State digest: access through the usual print process.

3.  Secondary Authority: Secondary resources such as the following will provide case authority:

    a.  *Ordinance Law Annotations* in print or electronic format through WestlawNext.

    b.  Treatises such as:

        (1)  E. McQuillin, *Law of Municipal Corporations*; or

        (2)  *Antieau on Local Government Law.*

4.  Update cases through appropriate *Shepard's* volumes.

## [b]  Electronic Version

1.  Locate interpretive cases through Lexis Advance or WestlawNext by accessing state cases.

2.  Consult a secondary source such as *Antieau on Local Government Law* through Lexis Advance or *Ordinance Law Annotations* through WestlawNext.

3.  Update any relevant cases through *Shepard's* on Lexis Advance or KeyCite on WestlawNext.

## [c]  Internet Version

Consult Fastcase or Casemaker state libraries for any interpretive cases. Update any such decisions through the Fastcase Bad Law Bot or Casemaker's Casecheck+.

## MUNICIPAL CODE CHECKLIST

Analyze the facts according to the TAPP rule.

**Print Version:**

1. Use the key words and phrases in the code index in print. Caveat: be sure it is the index for ordinances and not for the city charter.

2. Read the relevant section.

3. Note the page number and the supplement number or date at the bottom of the page.

4. Use the checklist sheets, usually located at the front of the volume, to determine whether the information is current or the most recent date indicated on the website.

5. Find interpretive case law by:

    a. State digest to access through the usual case search process;

    b. Secondary sources such as a treatise; or

    c. *Antieau on Local Government Law* or *Ordinance Law Annotations, Law of Municipal Corporations.*

6. Update by using the appropriate state volumes of *Shepard's.*

**Electronic Version:**

1. Consult the code through the cite website or code publishing companies. Use either the charter or the code index.

2. Note the currency of the provision.

3. Locate interpretive cases through the state cases components of Lexis Advance or WestlawNext.

4. An alternative for cases is a secondary source such as *Antieau on Local Government Law* on Lexis Advance or *Ordinance Law Annotations* on WestlawNext.

5. Update any applicable cases through *Shepard's* on Lexis Advance or KeyCite on WestlawNext.

**Internet Version:**

1. Consult the code through the cite website or code publishing companies' websites, Fastcase, or Casemaker.

2. Note currency of the provision.

3. Locate interpretive decisions, if any, through Fastcase or Casemaker and update through the Fastcase Bad Law Bot or Casemaker's Casecheck+.

## G.  ADDITIONAL TIPS

1. Consult all relevant state websites for information regarding state and local lawmakers and the state legislative processes.

2. Lexis Advance and WestlawNext provide access to selected legislative materials, as well as access into state judges' decisions on specific issues and docket information.

3. Secondary Sources, such as law review articles and media accounts, can provide important context for state and local legislation.

# Chapter 8

# STATE ADMINISTRATIVE RESEARCH

## A.  ADMINISTRATIVE LAW ORGANIZATION

The administrative function of the states is similar to that at the federal level. State agencies exercise power delegated to them through the governor or the state legislature. As government grows more complex at all levels, states require expanded administrative organization. The legal researcher should be aware of the daily importance of state administrative operations and be ready to locate any materials relevant to legal problems at the state level.

### [1]  Official Sources

State administrative materials, like their federal counterparts, take many forms. The governor's office issues orders and directives that will affect the operation of state agencies. State agencies issue licenses, orders, decisions, and rules interpreting and enforcing state statutes. Once again, these rules generally have the greatest impact of all administrative functions, and the alert researcher will be sure to check for the existence of such provisions. These provisions, however, do not exist in a vacuum and, like federal rules and regulations, are subject to interpretation by state and even federal courts. All research into state rules, then, will include the extra steps of finding any interpretive decisions, from state agencies and/or state and federal courts.

This process is complicated by the fact that publication of state administrative materials sometimes can be chaotic at best and nonexistent at worst. In addition, the pattern of publication is inconsistent from state to state. A few general statements, however, can be made about official publication of state rules and regulations. They generally appear first in a state "register" similar to the *Federal Register.* Such registers may be issued on a weekly, biweekly, or monthly basis, and some have no indexing system. The *Texas Register*, for example, is published weekly and includes proposed rules and regulations, items from the Governor, changes in or repeals of existing state rules, as well as a summary of state statutes enacted and summaries of attorney general opinions. The *Texas Register* includes annual and quarterly indices, available in print and online at the Secretary of State's website: www.sos.state.tx.us/texreg.

Every state now has an official administrative code arranged by subject matter. For example, the *Texas Administrative Code (T.A.C.)* is published annually by West for the state in 16 titles with 50 ultimately projected. Each title is divided into parts, chapters, subchapters, and sections. Every title contains rules still in force, incorporating new provisions and deleting those revoked, supported by a one-volume index or online at:

sos.state.tx.us/tac and updated continuously. Updating patterns for the codes will vary from state to state.

## [2]  Unofficial Sources

### [a]  Print Version

State administrative materials are generally published by the state or by official state sanction. There are some unofficial sources, however, that provide explanations of these materials. A good source for determining how each state's administrative documents are published and updated is William H. Manz's *Guide to State Legislation, Legislative History, and Administrative Materials.* This guide provides print and electronic sources of administrative information for all states, identifies the sources available and their update procedures, and includes addresses of the Secretary of State and other pertinent officials. The most useful tool, however, for descriptions of state agencies is a manual produced by most state governments similar to the *U.S. Government Manual.* The *Texas State Directory* (txdirectory.com), for example, appears annually in print and online and includes addresses and phone numbers for all branches of state and local government. This is the best source to use when information is needed about a particular agency or its rules. In addition, most state agencies now have their own websites.

### [b]  Electronic Version

Lexis Advance and WestlawNext provide coverage of a number of state administrative codes, such as the *Texas Administrative Code*, as well as state registers, such as the *Texas Register.*

### [c]  Internet Version

Internet access to all states' administrative codes is available at whpgs.org/f.htm, arranged by state name in alphabetical order. The Texas Administrative Code appears at the Secretary of State's website and is updated as of the current date, so there is no need to consult the print version, or its update process. The Texas Secretary of State's website is accessible at sos.state.tx.us/texreg. Fastcase provides access to the Texas Administrative Code and most other state codes. Casemaker's library includes all 50 state administrative codes.

# B.   STATE RULE AND REGULATION LOCATION METHODS

The methods of finding state rules and regulations depend upon the organization of each state's administrative code. For the purposes of this discussion, the *Texas Administrative Code*, is used as the model.

---

**LOOKING FOR A STATE RULE OR REGULATION?**

Use one of the following methods:

1.   Descriptive Word Method; or

2.   Topic Method.

---

**EXAMPLE:** An organization dedicated to the memory of Confederate soldiers seeks a Texas specialty license plate featuring the Confederate battle flag. Does the proposed plate conform to the state's requirements for such a plate procured through a third-party vendor?

## [1]   Descriptive Word Method

This is the most likely means of locating a state rule. Using the basic *Descriptive Word Method* that emphasizes the TAPP rule, go to the paperbound, annual *Texas Administrative Code* General Index or access the *T.A.C.* in electronic or internet format.

| | |
|---|---|
| Things: | license plates, motor vehicles |
| Acts: | specialty plate application |
| Persons: | private organization, third-party vendor |
| Places: | N/A |

Because the titles and chapter names are broad, the phrase "motor vehicles" as a subject leads to "license plates." A subcategory identifies "marketing of specialty license plates through a private vendor" at Title 43 Section 217.40.

## [2]   Topic Method

If the researcher has some familiarity with the titles in the state code, she may proceed directly to the relevant title and consult the individual subject index at the end of the title. Using this method, the researcher would go directly to Title 43 and turn to the subject index where the research process would continue in the manner applicable to the *Descriptive Word Method*. Once the state rule is located, it should be read carefully. Source notes follow the provision and explain the history of the rule, *i.e.*, when the rule was adopted or changed. Citations of Authority provide statutory or other authority for the rule, similar to enabling legislation at the federal level.

## C.   UPDATING A STATE RULE

To update state rules, follow the procedures listed below.

### [1]   Print Version

1.  Certification Date: Check the effectiveness date at the front of the volume or the front of any supplementary pamphlet.

2.  *Texas Register Index:* Depending upon the effectiveness date, check the quarterly *Texas Administrative Code Titles Affected* list arranged by title and section number. The quarterly list appears in the hard copy quarterly index to the *Texas Register.*

3.  Update: *Shepard's Texas Citations*, Code Volumes in hard copy and paper supplements in the *T.A.C.* section by Title and Section numbers. A Fifth Circuit case interprets the enabling legislation and regulation in the example problem as unconstitutional.

### [2]   Electronic Version

Lexis Advance and WestlawNext provide coverage of the *Texas Administrative Code* on a continuous updated basis, so there is no need to consult the Quarterly Index. Check the "currentness" icon instead. Shepardize on Lexis Advance or KeyCite on WestlawNext.

### [3]   Internet Version

The *Texas Administrative Code*, available at the Secretary of State's website, is continuously updated, so there is no need to continue to check the Quarterly Index. Consult Fastcase and Casemaker currency for each state's code.

## D.   FINDING AND UPDATING INTERPRETIVE CASES

Interpretive cases can be located in the following manner:

### [1]   Print Version

1.  Digest: Use the basic descriptive word method in the *Texas Digest* to locate interpretive cases because the *T.A.C.* provides no Notes of Decision.

2.  Reporter: Go to the appropriate reporter and read the case.

3.  Agency Decisions: Available officially from the agency on a sporadic basis.

4.  Update: The case in the appropriate *Shepard's* volumes.

## [2]  Electronic Version

1. Access relevant cases through citing references on Lexis Advance or WestlawNext provided with text of regulation.

2. Update any case through *Shepard's* on Lexis Advance or KeyCite on WestlawNext.

## [3]  Internet Version

Access agency decisions through individual agency website. Fastcase and Casemaker offer some administrative decisions.

---

**STATE RULES AND REGULATIONS CHECKLIST**

Analyze the fact situation according to the TAPP rule.

**Print Version:**

1. Locate the relevant rule or regulation by:

   a. The General Subject Method; or

   b. The Agency Name Method in the paperbound *T.A.C. General Index* issued annually.

2. Read the provision and check the Source Notes and Citations of Authority.

3. Update the rule or regulation by:

   a. Effectiveness date inside cover;

   b. *Texas Register Quarterly Index — T.A.C. Titles Affected.*

4. Find and update interpretive cases by:

   a. Update the *T.A.C.* Title and Code Section for interpretive decisions in the *Shepard's Texas Citations Code Volumes* and update pamphlets. Be sure to update any case through the relevant process for that source, e.g., *Shepard's.*

   b. The Descriptive Word Method in the *Texas Digest* or relevant state digest.

   c. Read the case in the appropriate reporter.

   d. Agency decisions issued sporadically by the state agency available through the agency..

**Electronic Version**

1. Read the provision located through Lexis Advance or WestlawNext and check the Source Notes and Citations of Authority.

2. To update the rule, note the currentness date.

3. Find and update interpretive cases through the citing references.

4. Update the cases with *Shepard's* on Lexis Advance or KeyCite on WestlawNext.

**Internet Version**

1. Consult the *T.A.C.* at the Secretary of State's website.

2. The code is updated daily at the website.

3. For interpretive court decisions, follow the print or electronic research processes described above, along with appropriate update processes.

4. For agency decisions, consult the relevant agency website.

5. Fastcase and Casemaker provide coverage of most administrative codes and some decisions.

## E.   ADDITIONAL TIPS

1. Determine whether there is a state guide to administrative agencies, such as the Texas State Directory. This is a good starting point to locate each agency's website and basic information about agency personnel.

2. Agency websites provide information explaining various processes. A state's Department of Motor Vehicles would likely provide a template for specialty license plates and explanations of how to propose such a plate and its process of approval.

3. If the research process involves agency decisions, check the agency website for those decisions or the links to the decisions through Lexis Advance or WestlawNext.

# Chapter 9

# SECONDARY SOURCE RESEARCH

## A.  SECONDARY SOURCE ORGANIZATION

Most of this guide has been dedicated to finding primary authority because that is the goal of the researcher. However, secondary authority can play a valid role in the research process. Furthermore, there is a hierarchy of secondary authority which will be discussed in this chapter.

Secondary authority is not the law itself; it is an analysis or explanation of primary authority. Although secondary authority should be cited infrequently in a legal memorandum or appellate brief, it can serve an important purpose in the research process.

There are two functions of secondary authority. The first is as a means of finding primary authority. As a research tool, the most valuable parts of these sources are the references because they provide the researcher with primary authority such as cases, statutes, or administrative codes, rules, and regulations. The second function of secondary authority is to provide insight into and background information on a particular problem. Thus, secondary authority can provide an overview of a subject or basic understanding to an area of law with which the researcher is unfamiliar.

Before using secondary authority, the researcher should ask certain questions about the advisability of using this type of source. The following checklist provides some guidance as to its value and the response to the researcher's mental query.

## CHECKLIST FOR USING SECONDARY AUTHORITY

1. Is there any primary authority from the jurisdiction where the case is being litigated?

    a. If this is a "case of first impression," then the court will be more receptive to reviewing the secondary authority.

    b. If the case presents a novel issue, then a source that weighs the merits of the issue is helpful.

2. Is secondary authority being used as a substitute for primary authority?

    a. If yes, then do not use it.

    b. If no, then it may be used to bolster the legal argument.

3. Is the secondary authority merely repetitive of the primary sources that are being used?

    a. If yes, then delete the reference to it.

    b. If no, then use it sparingly.

4. Will the source aid the court in its interpretation of primary authority?

    a. If yes, then it may be used, particularly if it is a new area of law or one where there has not been much litigation.

    b. If no, then it is irrelevant.

5. Is emphasis and a place of prominence given to secondary authority in the legal memorandum or appellate brief?

    a. If yes, then reassess its use because too great an emphasis is being given to it.

    b. If no, then use it wisely and sparingly.

6. Is there a proper foundation or predicate for the secondary source? Corollary issues to this point include the following questions:

    a. Is the source reliable?

        i. The quality of the product depends on the reputation and skill of the author.

        ii. It also depends on the reputation of the publisher, *i.e.*, for accuracy, etc.

    b. Is there contradictory primary authority?

        i. Court opinions, statutes, or the constitution will control.

7. If the secondary source is critical of a recent decision which has charted a new line of reasoning or has incorrectly applied the law, then there may be a valid role for the commentary.

## B.   HIERARCHY OF SECONDARY AUTHORITY

All secondary authority is *not* created equal! There are differences in these sources both in the weight of their authority and the likelihood of finding pertinent information. However, a typical reaction of a novice researcher is to use the first source without analyzing why that source is appropriate or inappropriate. It is the goal of this chapter to provide some insight on the use of secondary authority and why certain sources are more effective than others. Therefore, the discussion of secondary authority will consist of a brief description of that source; an itemization of the purposes of the particular material; some suggestions for appropriate ways to use the source within this hierarchy of secondary authority; and finally, a checklist describing the process of research for each source.

### [1]   Attorney General Opinions

### [a]   Description

Attorney General Opinions exist at both the federal and state levels of government. The Attorney General is the counsel for the government. Consequently, government officials can make a written request for a legal opinion on particular governmental matters. Three preliminary requirements must be met: (1) there must be an actual problem; (2) the problem must be presented to the Attorney General before the state or federal government is involved in civil or criminal litigation; and (3) it must be a question of law and not fact.

The Attorney General's opinions combine aspects of both primary and secondary authority. They are primary in the sense that they are opinions which are written like a judicial opinion and are supported by primary authority, and therefore, they are very persuasive. For example, there is a Supreme Court case where an auditor abused his discretion because he refused to follow an Attorney General Opinion. The opinions are also secondary in nature because they are only advisory opinions and are not binding or mandatory. Because of this dual status, Attorney General Opinions can be placed at the top of the secondary authority hierarchy.

### [b]   Purpose

Attorney General Opinions fulfill two purposes. First, through these opinions, the Attorney General gives legal advice to the President or Governor, as the case may be, or to the legislature and administrative agencies. Second, the Attorney General construes statutes and interprets judicial decisions and administrative regulations, particularly where the effect of the primary authority is uncertain.

### [c]   Use

When a researcher has a legislative problem, some consideration should be given to checking for an Attorney General Opinion. Opinions are an effective source of authority because: (1) they are written in response to specific inquiries by a government official about a current problem and not just an abstract or moot issue; (2) they are written in the style of a judicial opinion and supported with primary authority instead of being merely the "opinion" of the Attorney General; and (3) they are noted as cited references in *Shepard's Federal Citations*, *U.S. Administrative Citations*, and state citators.

## [d]  Location Method

**EXAMPLE #1:** On March 17, 2008, the Chair of the Ways and Means Committee requested that the Attorney General of Texas construe Texas Constitution article III as to whether a county may grant funds to a school district or charter school. On September 12, 2008, the Attorney General responded to the Chair of the Ways and Means Committee in Attorney General Opinion GA-0644. His opinion cited the Texas Constitution, statutory provisions, case law, and prior Attorney General Opinions. He concluded that Article III, § 52(a) of the Texas Constitution does not permit a county to gratuitously grant county funds to a school district or charter school, but it could make a payment if it accomplished a county purpose.

**EXAMPLE #2:** The Bexar County District Attorney asked the Attorney General whether the county clerk must accept for filing a "declaration of domestic partnership." The Attorney General responded on December 16, 1999 in Attorney General opinion JC-0156 by analyzing various statutory provisions including Family Code § 2.001, case law, and prior Attorney General Opinions. He stated that Texas recognizes only two forms of marriage, ceremonial and informal, and discussed each of those types. Texas does not recognize marriage between persons of the same sex whether they are ceremonial or informal. Declarations of domestic partnership are not documents required or permitted by law to be recorded. Therefore, the county clerks are not required to accept them for recording.

## [i]       Print Version

If the researcher is researching using the print version, there are four ways to find Attorney General Opinions. First, the researcher can check the individual index for the annual bound volume of opinions. Second, the researcher could check the digest of opinions if a digest is available. Third, if the researcher had already found a case or statute, then by Shepardizing it will show whether there was an Attorney General Opinion in its cited references. Fourth, the researcher could check secondary sources to find an opinion cited in the footnote.

There is no formal updating process for Attorney General Opinions. The index or digest would be the best ways to determine if additional opinions have been issued on a particular topic. As a general rule, Attorney General Opinions cannot be Shepardized.

## [ii]      Electronic Version

Attorney General Opinions can also be found through the electronic version, Lexis Advance and WestlawNext. Therefore, this problem could be resolved through either print or electronic versions.

## [iii]      Internet Version

Both Lexis Advance and WestlawNext have Attorney General Opinions that date back from 1791. This collection includes the official opinions of the U.S. Attorney General as well as the Opinions of the Office of Legal Counsel of the United States Department of Justice. Opinions from the Office of Legal Counsel begin in 1977 to current.

In addition, there are other websites that provide Attorney General Opinions. For example, Hein Online at www.heinonline.org has access to the State Attorney General Reports and Opinions for all 50 states as well as Puerto Rico and the Virgin Islands. How far back the collection goes varies with each state. For Texas, the collection is from 1840 to current.

---

### CHECKLIST FOR ATTORNEY GENERAL OPINIONS

**Print Version:**

1. To locate an Attorney General Opinion:

    a. Check the individual index for the annual bound volume of opinions;

    b. Check the digest of opinions if available;

    c. Shepardize any relevant case or statute to determine if an Attorney General Opinion is a cited reference *Shepard's*; or

    d. Check secondary sources to find an opinion cited in a footnote.

2. Read the relevant opinion in the bound volume:

    a. The opinions are reported in their full text in annual bound volumes.

    b. They are available on microfilm.

    c. They are available on Lexis Advance or WestlawNext.

    d. They are available on the Attorney General's website.

    e. They are also available through subscription based services such as Hein Online.

3. Update the Attorney General Opinions:

    a. There is no formal updating process. The index and digest are the best ways to determine if additional opinions have been issued on a topic.

    b. As a general rule, opinions cannot be Shepardized.

**Electronic Version:**

1. State Attorney General Opinions are available on Lexis Advance and WestlawNext.

2. Published opinions in the electronic version generally date back to 1791 and through current opinions.

---

3.  The United States Attorney General and the Office of Legal Counsel issue opinions in response to questions by either the President or the heads of the executive departments. Opinions of the Office of Legal Counsel are available from 1977 to current.

**Internet Version:**

1.  The Attorney General of each state has a website. Generally, the opinions of the Attorney General can be found on the official website.

2.  Hein Online also has Attorney General Opinions for all 50 states, Puerto Rico, and the Virgin Islands, but the beginning date varies for each state.

3.  Hein Online also provides access to the United States Attorney General Opinions and Opinions of the Office of Legal Counsel.

## [2]  *Restatements*

### [a]  Description

The *Restatements* of the law were begun in 1923 by the American Law Institute to simplify the case law by providing a clear and systematic restatement of it. It was the hope of the drafters of the *Restatement, First Series,* that the volumes would serve as a substitute for the codification of the law. However, this hope never became a reality.

*Restatements* provide the reader with a "black letter" statement of the law, an explanatory comment, examples of the principles, and variations of them. *Restatement, Second Series,* states new trends in the common law and will advocate what the rule will be or should be. In addition, the *Restatements* can be a good research tool. They provide case authority for the statements and cross references to West's topics and key numbers, as well as *A.L.R.* annotations.

Moreover, the *Restatements* have had an impact on the courts. Of all the types of commentaries, the *Restatements* are the most respected. This is evident by several series that are published for the purpose of citing cases that have applied or interpreted the *Restatements.* For example, West published a series called *Restatement in the Courts* until 1977. A few of the *Restatements* have been updated since that time. Since 1976, *Shepard's* has published a separate citator for the *Restatements.* In addition, separate volumes with annotations of court decisions have been provided in many states. For example, there are California annotations to the *Restatement of the Law of Torts.*

## [b]  Purpose

The *Restatements* fulfill several purposes. First, they provide an orderly statement of the common law. Second, they promote the classification and simplification of the law. Third, they provide suggestions for the law's adaptation to social needs and the better administration of justice. And finally, they provide a thorough review of the subject with cases on both sides of the issue as well as the drafters' commentary and illustrations.

## [c]  Use

Whether a *Restatement* is used in a research problem will be determined by the subject matter of the issue and the particular need that counsel has in the case. Concerning subject matter, the case must involve one of the ten topics that are included in the *Restatements*. This means that the researcher will be limited to the areas of agency, conflict of laws, contracts, foreign relations law, judgments, property, restitution, security, torts, and trusts. An additional limitation is that they are not mandatory or binding on the court because they lack legislative sanction. Concerning the needs of counsel, one might use the *Restatements* to: (1) support an argument that advocates either social change or an improvement to the justice system; (2) support an argument by experts within a particular field; or (3) support an argument where the court is faced with a case of first impression.

The effectiveness of the *Restatements* has varied from field to field. However, overall they have been very successful and have had considerable influence on the court. The publication itself has been accepted largely because of the intellectual scrutiny that has been given to each section of the *Restatements*. This acceptance primarily has been due to the scholarship of the authors and the publication. For instance, the authors include either well known scholars in the field or outstanding members of the judiciary.

## [d]  Location Method

**EXAMPLE:** Briner brought a cause of action against Hyslop for injuries sustained as a result of the negligent conduct of the corporation's employee. The issue was whether the corporation should be liable for punitive damages if it could have prevented the wrongful conduct of its employee.

This was a case of first impression in Iowa. Therefore, counsel needs to present persuasive authority that the corporation should not only be liable for the hiring and training of its employees, but it should also be held responsible where it could have prevented the employee's wrongful conduct.

### [i]          Print Version

It would be appropriate for the researcher to search the *Restatement of Torts 2d* for a solution to this case of first impression. The appropriate provision of the *Restatement of Torts 2d* can be found by using the Index for the *Restatement of Torts 2d* or by *Topic Method* by checking the Table of Contents for that Restatement. A more circuitous method would be by checking other secondary sources such as periodicals in the appropriate indices. The researcher would have to read and update the provision through pocket parts which have been available since 1976 or Shepardize the provision in *Shepard's Restatement of the Law Citations*.

In an actual case of *Briner v. Hyslop*, 337 N.W.2d 858 (Iowa 1983), the Iowa Supreme Court adopted the *Restatement* view and held the *Restatement* rule is the proper rule to apply when determining corporate liability for punitive damages for the acts of an employee. The opinion is also a good research tool because it lists the cases in states that have adopted the rule and those which have not.

### [ii]          Electronic Version

This problem could also be resolved through the electronic version. Both Lexis Advance and WestlawNext have a *Restatement* file. Lexis Advance, however, only carries the current series.

### [iii]          Internet Version

Both WestlawNext and Hein Online have the entire set of *Restatement* titles including the titles currently in effect, earlier versions of the titles, and tentative drafts.

## CHECKLIST FOR THE *RESTATEMENTS*

**Print Version:**

1. Find the *Restatement* provision by using:

    a. The General Index for the first series;

    b. The Individual Index for both series by individual subjects;

    c. The Topic Method by checking the Table of Contents for each *Restatement*; and

    d. Other secondary sources by checking for periodicals in the appropriate indices.

2. Read the relevant provision in the bound volumes.

3. Review the aids that are available such as the explanatory comments, illustrations, court citations, and cross references.

4. If the *Restatements* are used as a research tool for case authority, be sure to read the cases themselves and Shepardize them in the appropriate citator.

5. Update the information:

    a. *First Series:* See the appendices in the *Second Series.*

    b. Prior to 1977: See *Restatement in the Courts.*

    c. Since 1976: See the pocket parts in the *Second Series.*

6. Update the provision in *Shepard's Restatement of the Law* Citations in print or on Lexis Advance or KeyCite on WestlawNext.

**Electronic Version:**

1. The current *Restatements* are available on both Lexis Advance and WestlawNext.

2. Lexis Advance only has the current series, but WestlawNext has the current series as well as the earlier series and tentative drafts.

**Internet Version:**

1. The American Law Institute (ALI) website has a catalog of its publications including the *Restatements.*

2. Hein Online has the current series as well as the earlier series and tentative drafts. Online access is on a subscription only basis.

## [3]   Law Review Articles

### [a]   Description

Law reviews are produced by major American law schools and have been in existence since the mid-1800s. Articles are divided into three categories depending on the author. For example, lead articles are written by scholars and practitioners who do an extensive analysis of a subject. Notes and Comments are written by law students. "Comments" are generally longer and provide more depth than a student case "Note."

### [b]   Purpose

Law review articles fulfill several purposes. First, they provide a serious analysis of current legal issues, particularly judicial opinions. There is also some coverage of statutory provisions and administrative regulations. Second, they provide historical research. Articles will generally trace the history of the case law in that particular area of law. Third, articles may incorporate empirical studies or interdisciplinary aspects of legal problems. Fourth, they help to formulate legal policy arguments. Finally, they provide a research tool for cites to both primary and secondary sources. Typically, law review articles are rich in footnotes that cite to both primary and secondary authority.

### [c]   Use

Law review articles are helpful if the research involves case authority, particularly if the research focuses on a new area of law, if a recent or controversial case is relevant, or if inter-disciplinary research is needed. Law review articles have proven an effective source of authority because: (1) the editorial board exercises control over the acceptance of the articles, which ensures serious scholarship; and (2) they provide the most thorough discussion of new legal developments and issues.

### [d]   Location Method

**EXAMPLE #1:** John Miles worked at a nuclear power plant for five years. During that time, he was exposed to radiation and subsequently died. His widow seeks your advice on the liability of the plant operators and the damages she can obtain for his death.

### [i]      Print Version

For the print version, there are two ways to locate a law review article. One method focuses on the general subject matter; in this instance, the general subject matter is liability for nuclear accidents which is an emerging area of the law. The second method of finding a law review article involves research through case names such as *Silkwood v. Kerr-McGee Corporation*, which is the leading case in the area. Using the Index's Table of Cases, this case could lead to numerous law review articles. Law review articles are also available on the electronic version which will be discussed below.

**EXAMPLE #2:** The researcher wants to find law review articles on the federal Defense of Marriage Act (DOMA) and same sex marriage. Because the researcher does not know the name of a case, the general subject index would have to be used. The researcher would find law review articles on both the Defense of Marriage Act and same sex marriage.

## [ii]      Electronic Version

Both Lexis Advance and WestlawNext have legal periodicals. Although it is not comprehensive, there is a constantly growing number of law journals and American Bar Association (A.B.A.) publications that are being added to the databases. The databases usually go back to the 1980's. But both Lexis Advance and WestlawNext continue to add journals and related materials to the database.

## [iii]      Internet Version

On the Internet, the researcher might try the electronic equivalent to the *Index to Legal Periodicals and Books* which indexes more than 750 English-language legal periodicals and now goes back to 1908. That site is www.hwwilson.com/databases/legal. htm. Legaltrac is the electronic equivalent of the *Current Law Index* and indexes approximately 900 English-language legal periodicals. That site is www.gale.com/ but it is on a subscription basis. Hein Online is another subscription based resource that is providing comprehensive access to hundreds of journals from the very first issue as well as American Bar Association Journals and international journals. This site is www.heinonline.org. Many law schools are printing both a print copy and web copy of their journal. Other excellent sources are Legal Journals on the Web, FindLaw at www.findlaw.com, and WashLaw Web at www.washlaw.edu/.

---

### CHECKLIST FOR LAW REVIEW ARTICLES

**Print Version**

1. Find the law review article by:

    a. The *Index to Legal Periodicals (I.L.P.)* through its listing by:

        i. Subject/author;

        ii. Table of cases commented upon;

        iii. Table of statutes commented upon; or

        iv. Book reviews.

    b. The *Current Law Index (C.L.I.)* began in 1980 and indexes more periodicals than the *I.L.P.* Access to the article cites is the same as the *I.L.P.*:

        i. Subject index;

        ii. Author/title index;

        iii. Table of cases commented upon;

        iv. Table of statutes commented upon; or

       v.   Book reviews.

    c.   Law review articles can also be found on Lexis Advance and WestlawNext.

    d.   On the Internet, there are websites which correlate to the I.L.P. and the C.L.I. These can be found at www.hwwilson.com/databases/legal.htm or www.gale.com/ which is available on a subscription basis. Hein Online at www.heinonline.org is another subscription based resource.

2.   Read the article, carefully examining:

    a.   The text for policy arguments, historical information, and analysis; and

    b.   The footnotes for references to other primary and secondary authority.

3.   Read, analyze, and update the information that is found in the text and footnotes.

4.   *Shepard's Law Review Citations* provides a means to update the information by listing courts and other law reviews that have cited the article. This can be done through *Shepard's* in print.

**Electronic Version**

1.   Both Lexis Advance and WestlawNext have legal periodicals such as law journals and American Bar Association (A.B.A.) publications.

2.   There are limitations in both the number of journals that are available and how far back they are available.

3.   Updating can also be done through *Shepard's* on Lexis Advance or KeyCite on WestlawNext.

**Internet Version**

1.   Indices for law journal articles are available on the Internet. For example, Legaltrac is the online version of the *Current Law Index*.

2.   Hein Online is a subscription based resource to find and read law journal articles.

3.   FindLaw and WashLaw also provide Internet access to many journals. In addition, some law schools now have their journal available on the school's website.

## [4]  Treatises

### [a]  Description

Historically, treatises have been in existence since the 15th century. However, modern treatises are expositions on the case law and legislation. Treatises focus on a particular, narrow area of the law such as *Blashfield Automobile Law and Practice* or

*Couch on Insurance*, 3d. As a result, they are more comprehensive than some other forms of secondary authority such as an encyclopedia.

In addition, the term "treatise" refers to different forms of commentary. There are both *single* volume and *multi-volume* sets; there are *hornbooks*, which are student texts that introduce the terms and concepts of a particular legal field; *monographs*, which are one volume in length, narrow in scope, and are rarely supplemented; *practice guides*, which are designed for the practitioner in a particular area of law; and *handbooks for laymen*, which are very general in nature and include simplified instructions for conducting legal business.

In addition, there are a variety of "looseleaf" services. Traditionally, looseleaf services were print versions and on specialized topics such as labor relations or tax law. They are in binders and the pages can be replaced or added to at regular intervals to remain current. The benefit is that they can be kept very current with usually weekly updates. In addition, they have a wide variety of primary and secondary authority which can be found in one place. But a potential disadvantage is that a librarian needs to take out the old pages and insert new pages which can be time-consuming. Like other treatises, looseleaf services can be in single or multi-volume sets. Looseleaf services can be either in a newsletter format or an interfiled style. An example of a newsletter type form is the *United States Law Week* that contains new United States Supreme Court opinions, docketing and other information. With the interfiled type of looseleaf, there are no pamphlets but individual pages replace the outdated pages in the set. Included in the packet are filing instructions as to which pages are to be removed and the new ones inserted. An example of an interfiled looseleaf service is the *Standard Federal Tax Reporter* by Wolters Kluwer CCH. Bloomberg BNA and CCH are two of the major publishers of looseleaf services and these sets can now be found in print or electronic versions.

Although the forms may vary, there are certain common characteristics to most treatises. For instance, treatises are written in narrative style with a general discussion of the point. This information is supported by footnotes with references to both primary and secondary authority. Charts and appendices are also common in treatises. All of these materials can be located through an index at the back of the volume.

## [b]  Purpose

Treatises will: (1) summarize the historical developments in that particular field of law; (2) analyze and explain any inconsistencies in the law; (3) predict future changes to the law; and (4) provide practical insights into courtroom procedure and methods of conducting business.

## [c]  Use

Treatises can be a valuable research tool. For example, a treatise gives the researcher the perspective of the author on a particular subject; it provides interpretation of statutes and case law; it is a means of finding cases; and it presents the general principles, exceptions, and variations in an area of law.

The disadvantage is that the quality of the treatise depends on the author and his reputation, knowledge, and skill. The quality will also depend on the publisher and the accuracy of cites and text.

## [d]  Location Method

**EXAMPLE:** The issue to be resolved is whether a parody falls within parameters of the "fair use" doctrine under the copyright law.

Due to the nature of the problem, it may be advisable for the researcher to begin with a treatise if the researcher is unfamiliar with the general terms of copyright law. The following checklist will demonstrate the research procedure.

## [i]  Print Version

Finding a treatise has changed over the years. The traditional method of using a print version of a card catalog have faded away to online versions at the law library. They can be searched by title, subject, or author's name. Some treatises are well-known and standards within the area of law. These may be recommended by other lawyers or researchers.

Looseleaf services can be found both in print and online. Arlene L. Eis has written a reference work entitled *Legal Looseleafs in Print* that is published annually by Infosources Publishing and provides information on locating relevant looseleafs. It lists over 3,600 looseleafs by topic, title, and publisher. It indicates whether the looseleaf is available in electronic format. There is also an electronic version available through Infosources Publishing on a subscription basis at http://www.infosourcespub. com/book5.cfm.

Once a treatise is found, the researcher can find the relevant specific section by a subject index at the back of the book or in a separate volume or index if it is a multi-volume treatise. The section could also be found through the table of contents in the beginning of the book or a table of cases or statutes if available in the treatise and the researcher already has a case or statute.

The relevant section must be read with particular attention to the footnotes which will cite cases, statutes, *Restatements*, or other secondary authority. One of the benefits of a treatise is getting the expert commentary or analysis by a respected author.

Once the relevant section is read, it must be updated. This is usually done through a pocket part in the back of the book. Be sure to look at the date on the pocket part. Most treatises should have an annual pocket part. If primary authority such as cases or statutes are found, then they must be read and updated.

## [ii]  Electronic Version

There are electronic means of finding treatises. Both Lexis Advance and WestlawNext have some treatises online. For example, there are some California materials such as Witkin's *Summary of California Law*, Witkin & Epstein's *Criminal Law* (3d ed.), Witkin's *California Procedure* (5th ed.), and Witkin's *California*

*Evidence* (4th ed.). It is very helpful if treatises are available, but the problem is that there is only a limited number of treatises available online.

Some of the looseleaf services are available electronically. The newsletter type of looseleafs were the first to be available electronically while the interfiled types are more problematic for this type of search. Bloomberg BNA has made the *United States Law Week* available online, although it may be faster or easier to get the information through the Supreme Court website or Lexis Advance and WestlawNext, particularly if the researcher does not have subscription access to Bloomberg BNA.

## [iii]        Internet Version

Through the Internet, there are other means of searching for a treatise. Harvard Law School has legal guides including "Legal Treatises by Subject" which is available at http://libguides.law.harvard.edu/legaltreatises. It provides a selective list of legal treatises that are arranged by 54 major subject headings such as administrative law, education law, insurance law, and securities law.

IndexMaster at www.indexmaster.com is a subscription based service for finding treatises and has over 8,000 titles. IndexMaster offers a service that links the web-based library catalog system directly to the specific Index and/or table of contents of any IndexMaster title. This can be done in one of two ways. The first way is to match IndexMaster titles against the researcher's Library's titles by using an OPAC or an ISBN list that the researcher provides. Any matches that are found cost $1 per title and they are re-run every six months to ensure the most up-to-date links. A second option is that IndexMaster will provide a complete list of all of IndexMaster's holdings by title, author, publisher, ISBN (where applicable) as well as a hyperlink to it. The list is updated every six months. The cost for this service is $250 per year, which includes the updates.

---

### CHECKLIST FOR A TREATISE

**Print Version**

1.  Find a treatise by:

    a.  The online or print "catalog" at the law library under title, subject, or author's name; or

    b.  Recommendation of others.

2.  Evaluate the quality of the treatise by:

    a.  The reputation and stature of the author;

    b.  The reputation of the publisher;

    c.  The purpose and originality of the work;

    d.  The research aids that are available; and

    e.  The frequency of the supplementation.

3.  Find the relevant section in the treatise by:

a. The subject index at the back of the book or possibly in separate volumes if the treatise is a multi-volume set;

b. The table of contents in the beginning of the book; or

c. The table of cases or statutes if you already have one good case or statute.

4. Read the section.

5. Review the footnotes for cases and other relevant information.

6. Update the information. Generally this is through an annual pocket part. However, be sure to check the date on the pocket part to see how recent it is so that the material can be updated from that point through other conventional updating procedures.

7. Read the relevant cases or statutes from the text or footnotes of that material.

8. Update all relevant information in the appropriate volumes of *Shepard's* citators in print or on Lexis Advance or KeyCite on WestlawNext.

**Electronic Version**

1. There are a limited number of treatises that are available on Lexis Advance or WestlawNext.

2. Updated materials are usually integrated into the text so that the researcher is viewing the current materials.

**Internet Version**

1. The researcher is able to find what treatises are available through Internet sources. For example, Harvard Law School has a legal guide for treatises. IndexMaster is a subscription based service for finding treatises.

2. The treatise itself is generally not available through the Internet.

## [5]  Legal Encyclopedias

### [a]  Description

Legal encyclopedias, while valuable as a reference, have little weight in persuading a court to accept a particular position. There are several reasons for this view. Generally speaking, legal encyclopedias place emphasis on case authority, but there is little treatment of statutory law. This factor alone is a great limitation on the resource and may present a distorted picture of the subject matter. In addition, the articles are not written by well-known scholars or jurists, and therefore, the reputation of the authors does not have the impact that a treatise by an expert in the field might have. Furthermore, in an effort to give a clear and concise statement of the law, encyclopedias tend to provide over-simplified and generalized treatment of the subject.

There are three types of legal encyclopedias. The first type is a *general* encyclopedia which discusses all American law. Examples of this type are *Corpus Juris Secondum*

*(C.J.S.)* by Thomson Reuters and *American Jurisprudence (Am. Jur.)*, formerly by Lawyers Cooperative Publishing, now by Thomson Reuters. Although the format and research procedure for the two encyclopedias is virtually the same, there are major differences in the approach between the two publications. For example, *C.J.S.* purports to cover all cases, references are to its topic and key numbers, and there is limited statutory coverage. On the other hand, *Am. Jur.* uses only selected cases which it feels are the most important, it cites to its Total Client Service Library and Research References, which has more secondary sources, it has more statutory coverage, and it produces a *Desk Book* as a helpful quick reference to an array of information and data that might be needed by the practitioner such as historical documents, international agreements and organizations, federal government and agencies, national statistics, and research and practice aids. The *New Topic Service* provides new areas of law in a binder until they can be placed in the set.

The second type of encyclopedia is a *local* encyclopedia. These encyclopedias focus on a specific state. Fifteen states have encyclopedias. An example of a local encyclopedia is *Michie's Jurisprudence of Virginia and West Virginia*, published by LexisNexis. The coverage and philosophy of these publications will differ depending on the publisher.

There are some advantages to the local encyclopedias over the general ones. For example, the researcher will find only the law of the jurisdiction that he is interested in and not law for all of the states. Furthermore, there tends to be greater coverage of statutory law in the local encyclopedias than in the general ones. At best, the general encyclopedia will state that a statute may apply or, as in *Am. Jur.*, the publisher will note selected statutes. Also, the local encyclopedias usually provide a table of statutes cited for ease in locating them in the text.

In addition to the local encyclopedias, the publishers may also produce state-specific supplementary materials for the practitioner which parallel their encyclopedias or digests. For example, West publishes an outline or summary of the law which is more limited than the encyclopedias such as *Summary of California Law* and *Encyclopedia of Mississippi Law* (formerly *Summary of Mississippi Law*). Thomson Reuters produces the state practice series, which are generally multi-volume sets but which are not as comprehensive as the encyclopedias. Examples of these include *California Practice, Massachusetts Practice Series, New Jersey Practice*, and *Louisiana Civil Law Treatise Series*. And finally, several publishers issue what are known as state law finders which try to consolidate access to both primary and secondary authority on a subject. Examples of this type of publication include *Illinois Law Finder, Massachusetts Law Finder, New York Law Finder, Pennsylvania Law Finder*, and *Texas Law Finder*.

The third type of encyclopedia is a special interest encyclopedia. Thomson Reuters' Total Client Service Library produces what the company calls "how-to-do-it" books. For instance, *Am. Jur. Trials* is a special series that is an encyclopedic guide to modern trial practices, procedures, and strategies. It provides commentary by an expert in the field, cross references to other sources, checklists of questions to ask or things to do, sample forms or diagrams, and illustrations on how to compile evidence.

## [b]  Purpose

The purpose of these encyclopedias is two-fold. First, they give a general discussion of the law. Depending on the type of encyclopedia, it will be a discussion of all American law or the law of a particular state. Second, they briefly summarize the rule of law and support the proposition with case authority and other cross references.

## [c]  Use

Legal encyclopedias are not an effective source to cite in a legal memorandum or an appellate brief. The court gives this form of secondary authority little weight because they are not scholarly writing and do not provide a detailed analysis or authoritative statement of the law.

In spite of these limitations, the legal encyclopedia can be a valuable research tool because it is a good starting point for legal research. If the researcher wants background information on an unfamiliar area of law, or wants a general overview of the subject, or needs a narrative introduction to basic concepts, then an encyclopedia is a good place to begin. In addition, the legal encyclopedia is a good tool for finding case authority for a proposition; however, the limitation of not having comprehensive legislative materials must be kept in mind. Encyclopedias also have definitions of important legal terms and legal maxims. Although it is not as comprehensive as a legal dictionary, the legal encyclopedia includes definitions of most important legal terms or legal maxims. Thus, if the research problem involves a definition, the encyclopedia might be one place to look.

## [d]  Location Method

**EXAMPLE #1:** Your clients, Joe and Ima Spectator, seek your advice concerning personal injuries they received while watching a baseball game when a foul ball struck them. Joe regularly attended games at the stadium and had season tickets for seats that were in the unscreened section behind first base. Ima was both uninterested in baseball and unknowledgeable of the possible dangers lurking in and about playing fields. The issue is whether the owners of the stadium are liable for the injuries sustained by Joe and Ima Spectator.

If a state were listed in the problem, then the researcher would start with a local encyclopedia such as *Texas Jurisprudence*. Because no state has been listed in this problem, use *Am. Jur. 2d*. This problem could be run through either a national or local encyclopedia. How the publisher catalogs the index may create differences in the key words and phrases that are used.

Due to the nature of the problem, this issue could be resolved through a case. Because the researcher is looking for a case, the fact analysis should follow that which was discussed under finding a case. The analysis might be as follows:

| Parties: | spectators, patrons, owner, team, proprietor of sports arena |
| Places & Things: | baseball game, sports, amusement place, theatre, show, entertainment |
| Bases of Action: | negligence for failing to erect and maintain a screen, negligence for failing to warn of dangers, ignorance of potential dangers by the plaintiff |
| Defenses: | assumption of the risk, contributory negligence, duty of ordinary care |
| Relief Sought: | damages for negligence, medical expenses, court costs, attorney's fees |

In the analysis, the key words or phrases for *Am. Jur. 2d* are "baseball" and "personal injuries." These key words and phrases would lead the researcher to 27A Am. Jur. 2d *Entertainment and Sports Law* § 76 (2008).

**EXAMPLE #2:** In the problem concerning whether same-sex marriages are allowed under federal law, the researcher could also use an encyclopedia. Using the *Descriptive Word Method*, the words "marriage," "definition," and "same-sex" are key terms.

## [i]          Print Version

Use *Corpus Juris Secundum (C.J.S.)*. In the *Descriptive Word Index*, the word "marriage" and the subheading "definition" leads the researcher to the topic of Marriage § 1. The words "marriage" and the subheading of "same-sex marriages" in the Index leads the researcher to Marriage § 7.

Both sections should be checked. Marriage § 1 defines marriage in relevant part as "the civil status of one man and one woman . . . ." On the other hand, Marriage § 7 specifically discusses the status of same-sex marriages and the federal Defense of Marriage Act. Both sections cited cases, but § 7 also lists the *A.L.R.* reference to 1 A.L.R. Fed. 2d 1 which was found when the researcher was looking for a case in the Case Law Research chapter of this text.

The pocket part of the encyclopedia needs to be checked. In this example, the 2012 cumulative annual pocket part does not have anything for Marriage § 1, but there is an additional case in Marriage § 7. Any relevant cases that were found in this process must be read and Shepardized.

## [ii]          Electronic Version

Legal encyclopedias can also be found in the electronic versions. Both Lexis Advance and WestlawNext will reference to *C.J.S.* or *Am. Jur. 2d*. This could be either when you are searching for primary authority and there is a reference to one of the encyclopedias or through searching directly in those databases.

## [iii]    Internet Version

Unlike some Internet encyclopedias, legal encyclopedias are not on the Internet. In other primary or secondary materials on the Internet, the researcher might find a reference to a particular section in the legal encyclopedia.

---

### ENCYCLOPEDIA CHECKLIST

**Print Version**

1. Analyze the facts according to Parties, Places, Basis of the Action, Defenses, and Relief Sought.

2. Use the key words and phrases in the softbound General Index of the encyclopedia. Be sure to check any update pamphlets to the General Index.

3. Turn to the appropriate title in the encyclopedia.

4. Scan both the Title Index and the Title Table of Contents for specific sections to obtain additional information and to understand the organization of the title.

5. Read the relevant provision for an understanding of the law.

6. For interpretive case law:

   a. Check the Research References for digest topic and key number information if the encyclopedia is published by West; and

   b. Check the footnotes.

7. Update the information by using:

   a. The annual pocket part which will update both the text and the footnotes;

   b. The topic and key number in the relevant state digest which will provide more current information about recent cases; and

   c. The topic and key number in the advance sheets of the relevant reporter which will also provide a case update for within the last six weeks.

8. Read, analyze, and Shepardize all of the relevant cases. The researcher can use *Shepard's* in print or on Lexis Advance or KeyCite on WestlawNext. It should be noted that West states that complete citation and full history are provided for each case. However, this is not a substitute for updating in either *Shepard's* or KeyCite.

**Electronic Version**

1. Lexis Advance has *Am. Jur. 2d* and WestlawNext has both *C.J.S.* and *Am. Jur. 2d*.

2.  The researcher could find a section in the legal encyclopedias through a direct search into that particular database.

3.  Some local encyclopedias are also available online. The researcher can check the databases of Lexis Advance or WestlawNext to determine which ones are available.

**Internet Version**

1.  Legal encyclopedias are not on the Internet.

2.  In other primary or secondary materials on the Internet, the researcher might find a reference to a particular section in the legal encyclopedia.

## [6]  Legal Dictionaries

### [a]  Description

The legal dictionary has been in existence since the 16th century. The first legal dictionary was written by John Rastell in England for the purpose of defining 208 obscure terms. Today, there are several types of legal dictionaries.

The first type of legal dictionary is categorized as a law dictionary. Two leading law dictionaries are *Black's Law Dictionary* and *Ballentine's Law Dictionary*. Typical features of these dictionaries include: a pronunciation guide; definitions of both modern and ancient terms; definitions of both English and foreign terms; cites to court decisions if the definition is from a case; and cross references to other sources. The types of cross references that are included depend upon the publisher. For example, *Black's Law Dictionary* has references to the *Restatements*, U.C.C., statutes, and court rules. *Ballentine's Law Dictionary* refers the reader to *A.L.R.* and *Am. Jur.* Concerning the number of terms, the dictionaries have grown from 208 obscure phrases to over 50,000 terms in *Black's Law Dictionary* (10th ed. 2014).

The second type of legal dictionary is a judicial dictionary. This type is exemplified by the series *Words and Phrases*. This multi-volume set is published by West and contains an alphabetical listing of the word or phrase followed by an abstract of the court decision that defined the word. These abstracts look like the case abstracts that are found in the digests. This publication is updated by annual pocket part supplements. A words and phrases section can also be found in various digests and the advance sheets of the reporters.

The third type of legal dictionary is a specialized dictionary. This type focuses on one particular area of law. For example, Kase has written a *Dictionary of Industrial Property and Related Terms*.

## [b]  Purpose

The legal dictionary has two basic functions. The first is to aid legal research by: clarifying the complexity of legal terminology; providing accurate and precise use of words and phrases; and clarifying the nuances, subtleties, and ambiguities of language. The second goal of a legal dictionary is to define legal terms, phrases, and concepts that would not be found in an ordinary dictionary.

## [c]  Use

Dictionaries are essentially tools for resolving a definitional problem; they are rarely used as cited authority. Thus, if the researcher has a definitional problem, there are three types of sources that could be consulted. Which source the researcher uses will depend on the type of term that is in question and the author of the source.

## [d]  Location Method

**EXAMPLE:** The researcher wants to know the definition of marriage, specifically same-sex marriage and the federal Defense of Marriage Act (DOMA). Use *Black's Law Dictionary* (10th ed. 2014). Using the word "marriage," definitions are given for various subtopics such as same-sex marriage and the Defense of Marriage Act. In the following entries, cases and the statute are cited. In addition, other terms are suggested. The entries for same-sex marriage and the Defense of Marriage Act are as follows:

> The ceremonial union of two people of the same sex; a marriage between two women or two men. See U.S. v. Windsor, 133 S. Ct. 2675 (2013). Also termed gay marriage; homosexual marriage. Cf. Civil Commitment; Civil Union; Domestic Partnership.

> Defense of Marriage Act. A federal statute that (1) provides that no state can be required to recognize or give effect to same-sex marriages, (2) defines the term "marriage" for purposes of federal law as the union of a man and a woman as husband and wife, and (3) defines "spouse" for purposes of federal law as being only a person of the opposite sex. 1 USCA § 7; 28 USCA 1738C. The Defense of Marriage Act was enacted in response to the fear that if one state sanctioned same-sex marriages, other states might then have to give full faith and credit to those marriages. Key parts of the statute were invalidated in U.S. v. Windsor, 133 S. Ct. 2675 (2013).

### [i]     Print Version

It should be noted that beginning with the Seventh Edition of *Black's Law Dictionary*, Bryan Garner began as the editor. He is an expert and noted for his courses on legal writing, word usage, and the restyling of the federal rules. He has tried to make *Black's Law Dictionary* both more scholarly and more practical; the Seventh Edition was almost entirely rewritten with increased precision and clarity. In addition, hundreds of Roman-law terms were added that had been omitted from prior editions. Various appendices have been added at the end with things such as legal abbreviations, legal maxims, the Constitution of the United States, the Universal Declaration of Human Rights, members of the United States Supreme Court, and the federal circuit map.

### [ii]     Electronic Version

In the electronic version, it is also possible to get a definition of terms. For example, if the researcher does not understand a term while using WestlawNext, it is possible to get the relevant page in *Black's Law Dictionary*. It is also possible to find judicial definitions of words while using Lexis Advance or WestlawNext.

### [iii]     Internet Version

On the Internet, there are various websites that provide legal dictionaries. These include: Law.com at http://dictionary.law.com/ or Nolo's *Free Dictionary* at http://nolo.com/dictionary.

## DICTIONARY CHECKLIST

**Print Version**

1.  Determine which word or phrase is ambiguous.

2.  Use one of the following sources:

    a.  A law dictionary such as *Black's Law Dictionary* or *Ballentine's Law Dictionary*;

    b.  A judicial dictionary such as *Words and Phrases*;

    c.  A specialized dictionary if one exists for the topic. These could be located through the card catalog by checking the subject catalog;

    d.  A local encyclopedia; or

    e.  Possibly a general encyclopedia if the term could not be found in the local encyclopedia.

3.  Update the information if possible:

    a.  *Words and Phrases* can be updated through:

        i.   Annual pocket part supplement;

        ii.  Those digests that have a words and phrases section; and

        iii. The advance sheets of the reporter.

    b.  Encyclopedias can be updated through pocket parts.

4.  If the term has been defined by a court, then look up the case and cite the definition from the court's opinion.

5.  Update any cases in the appropriate *Shepard's* in print.

**Electronic Version**

1.  *Ballantine's Law Dictionary* is searchable on Lexis Advance. *Black's Law Dictionary* is searchable on WestlawNext.

2.  The researcher can also find judicial definitions of words while using Lexis Advance or WestlawNext.

3.  Update any cases through *Shepard's* on Lexis Advance or KeyCite on WestlawNext.

**Internet Version**

1.  There are several legal dictionaries that are available on the Internet. For example, the researcher can find definitions on Law.com and *Nolo's Free Dictionary*.

2.  Other legal and non-legal dictionaries are available online.

## [7]   Form Books

### [a]   Description

Many of the problems or transactions that occur in the practice of law are similar. This fact has led to the development of legal forms. Since the 18th century, lawyers have been able to purchase single printed forms at a legal stationers. As time went on, individual practitioners and law firms retained forms they had used in their practice so that they could be modified and reused in similar future transactions. Today, standard form books have become a major part of legal literature.

There are five types of form books. The first type is a general encyclopedic kind with extensive indices, annotations to cases, references to statutes and other primary sources, tax notes, cross references to other relevant materials, and regular pocket part supplementation. Examples of this multi-volume, encyclopedic type of a form book are *West's Modern Legal Forms*, *Am. Jur. Legal Forms*, and *Am. Jur. Pleading and Practice Forms*.

In addition to these major works, the second type of form book is a specialized form book which specializes in a particular subject of law. These form books are commonly found in areas such as real estate transactions, wills, and corporate practice.

The third type of form book may be part of the state practice guides as discussed under encyclopedias. The state practice guide forms are coordinated with the text material in the guide so that the practitioner has a handy reference to the text, acts, court rules, and forms. Two examples of this type of form book are *Douglas' Forms* (North Carolina) and *Virginia Forms*, both of which are published by LexisNexis.

The fourth type of form book is a statutory form book. The forms in these books are coordinated with the state codes. References are made to the code provision and its annotations. Their function is to meet the specific statutory requirements that are outlined in the code section.

The final type of form "book" has come into existence with the development of computer technology. Computer-assisted drafting, as it is called, is a means of storing and retrieving complete legal documents and forms. The American Bar Association has conducted studies and experiments about the feasibility of this type of word processing. In addition, numerous commercial firms such as Matthew Bender and Michie (both part of LexisNexis) have software programs to provide this type of information.

### [b]   Purpose

The purpose of form books is three-fold. First, they provide standard forms that can be used and re-used by practitioners. These forms can be divided into two categories: (1) forms of instrument, *i.e.*, forms that effectuate legal transactions such as contracts, wills, or leases; and (2) forms of practice, *i.e.*, forms that are part of the business before the courts or administrative agencies such as various motions, pleadings, or judgments. The second purpose of form books is to provide a practical dimension to the law. In other words, it is the "how-to-do-it" aspect of law practice. Finally, form books provide summaries of the law and checklists that give meaning and substance to the form.

## [c] Use

There is no argument that the use of form books is an important aid to office practice and that they are commonly used by practitioners. However, the researcher must keep in mind the advantages and disadvantages to using a form.

There are several advantages to using form books. First, they save tremendous time and effort. If a form has already been prepared, it saves the researcher's time in preparing a new document. The second advantage is a corollary of the first. The researcher has the benefit of using a standard document which incorporates the expertise of others, legal precedents, and statutory requirements. In other words, the researcher is not left alone to create the "perfect" document.

The third advantage of form books is that they are annotated, have notes on the tax consequences of a provision, and are keyed to applicable statutes. These research aids provide the assurance that the forms are correct and have been approved by the courts, legislature, or bar association. A final benefit is that they are frequently supplemented so that changes in the law are reflected in the forms.

In spite of these advantages, there are two disadvantages. These disadvantages are associated with the care that the researcher must use in copying a form. The first caveat is that wholesale copying of the form is dangerous. The form must be carefully and thoroughly read. Provisions that would be inappropriate or detrimental to the client must be removed and other language added. The second caveat is that modifications must be made for the specific facts and circumstances of each transaction. It would be a violation of professional responsibility for the researcher to disregard these caveats.

## [d] Location Method

**EXAMPLE:** A client comes to your office because he wants to purchase a condominium. He asks you to write a deed for the condominium. Where would you look to find such a form?

## [i]      Print Version

In a print version, a sample deed could be found in a form book by using either the Topic or Descriptive Word Method. The researcher must read the introductory materials, checklists, and other researches guides as well as to carefully and thoroughly read the appropriate form. It would be a major and costly mistake to wholesale copy the form without insuring that it meets the needs of the client or does not have clauses that could be very detrimental to the client Thus, the researcher would have to make appropriate changes in any paragraphs or words to tailor the form to the client's needs. Updating form books is through pocket parts which will give the up-to-date information on new forms, tax notes, how to use the forms, and other relevant information.

## [ii]     Electronic Version

In the electronic version, both Lexis Advance and WestlawNext provide forms. For example, *Am. Jur. Legal Forms 2d* has more than 22,000 transactional documents which include forms, clauses, and checklists business organizations, commercial transactions, estate planning and probate, land use and zoning, patents, real property, and workers' compensation. *Am. Jur. Pleading and Practice Forms Annotated* provides more than 43,000 forms covering every stage of both state and federal litigation such as notices, complaints, petitions, motions, answers, discovery forms, affidavits, subpoenas, orders, jury instructions, and judgments.

## [iii]    Internet Version

On the Internet, there are many websites that provide forms. For example,

* WashLaw at www.washlaw.edu/legalforms/ has links to state business forms, state tax forms, state company formation forms, real estate forms, contract forms, will forms, federal court forms, state court forms, legal forms, trademark forms, UCC forms, workers' compensation forms, department of labor law forms, and form databases such as Edgar, Findforms, ChooseLaw, HUD Forms, and Lectric Law Library.

* FindLaw also has a collection of forms at www.findlaw.com/16forms/collections.html including forms concerning particular issues, government forms, state corporate and business forms, state family law forms, and state tax forms.

* Lawyers.com at http://www.lawyers.com/site-search.html?s=forms has selected forms.

* Lectric Law Library's Law Practice Forms at http://www.lectlaw.com/form.html.

- Some law schools have begun to collect links to forms from both official and unofficial services. For example, a good source for government websites that have downloadable forms is the Uncle Sam website at the University of Memphis which is available at http://www.memphis.edu/govpub/forms.php. For example, there are forms for the Bureau of Alcohol, Tobacco and Firearms & Explosives or the Food and Drug Administration.

In addition, forms that are used by practitioners in particular states can be found in print, on Lexis Advance, WestlawNext, or on the web for free or a subscription. One example would be *West's Texas Forms 2d*. For a fee, there are also state specific forms from companies such as U.S. Legal Forms at http://www.uslegalforms.com or Legal-Zoom at http://www.legalzoom.com. LawInfo, a Thomson Reuters company, provides access to about 100 free forms in a variety of categories, but the researcher will be asked to register. LawInfo forms are available at http://legalforms.lawinfo.com/.

A word of caution: just as the researcher must carefully and thoroughly read and modify any forms in the print version, the same is true in the electronic version. In addition, it is critically important to trust the source where the researcher is getting the form. Lectric Law Library has properly put this warning at the beginning of its form section:

> *Exercise Extreme Caution* when using many of our free forms — or any legal material. While they may provide general ideas on format & content, validity requirements *can and do vary greatly from state to state.* Many *MUST be Properly Modified* for your own location and circumstances.[1]

---

[1] This warning is from Lectric Law Library at http://ww.lectlaw.com/form.html (emphasis in original). The company has also included a longer warning stating in part:

> Although we try to insure the Library's holdings are accurate and virus-free, we ONLY guarantee that it contains no intentional mistakes or defects and has no fraudulent, unlawful or improper purpose. Otherwise there is no guarantee made or implied about the accuracy, currency, usefulness, functionality, safety, toxicity or anything else regarding the Library or anything in it, near it, related to it, or connected with it in any way. Use it at your own risk!

*See* http://www.lectlaw.com/lll/faq-acc.html (emphasis in original).

## FORM BOOK CHECKLIST

**Print Version**

1. Find the relevant section in a form book by:

   a. Topic Method: Use the Topic Method if you know the general topic area where the form is likely to appear. Once in the appropriate volume and chapter, use the detailed outline at the beginning of the chapter to obtain the proper form.

   b. Descriptive Word Method: If you do not know where it might be located, then analyze your facts according to the TAPP rule and use those key words and phrases in the General Index. This analysis will provide the proper chapter and section number.

2. Read the introductory materials, checklists, and other research guides to become familiar with the law, requirements, and any caveats that the author may suggest.

3. Read carefully and thoroughly the appropriate form. Do not use a wholesale copy of the form.

4. Make appropriate changes in paragraphs or words to tailor the form to your client's needs.

5. Update the information by checking the pocket parts. The supplement will give up-to-date information on new forms, tax notes, how to use the forms, and other relevant information.

**Electronic Version**

1. Legal forms are available on Lexis Advance and WestlawNext.

2. In the electronic version, be careful to review any dates as to when the form was updated or any commentary or caveats that are given for using the form. Even with these warnings, counsel must use his/her own professional judgment and will ultimately be responsible for the content of the form.

**Internet Version**

1. Legal forms are available on a variety of websites.

2. As in other versions, be careful to review any dates as to when the form was updated, caveats that the company gives for using the form, and only go to sites that are reliable, trustworthy, and competent. Even with these warnings, counsel must use his/her own professional judgment and will ultimately be responsible for the content of the form.

## [8]  Legal Directories

### [a]  Description

There are various types of directories. Some directories compile a national list of attorney data, while others are specialized directories for specific fields of law, jurisdictional directories for state or regional areas, or judicial directories which list the national or regional information about judges. However, the most pertinent directory for the purposes of this book is *Martindale-Hubbell Law Directory*, and therefore, it will be the focus of this section.

### [b]  Purpose

*Martindale-Hubbell* serves two purposes. The first is to provide a listing of attorneys who have been admitted to the bar of any jurisdiction. This multi-volume set is published annually and lists attorneys alphabetically by state and city, by bar roster, and by law firms. In addition, the directory has a rating system whereby an attorney can be rated according to legal ability, ethical standards, professional reliability, and other such criteria. Attorneys may request not to have a rating.

The last volume of *Martindale-Hubbell* is the law digest volume of uniform acts. This volume is a comprehensive digest of laws from the states, federal government, and territories. It is compiled under approximately 100 major subject headings and up to 500 subheadings which the editors feel are the most useful to the legal profession. It also has notations about the forms of instrument that are used by that state or jurisdiction.

In 1990, Reed Elsevier, the parent company of LexisNexis, purchased Martindale-Hubbell. In October 2013, Reed Elsevier entered into a joint venture with Internet Brands, LLC, and by March 2014, the joint venture was completed. This resulted in the combination of Martindale-Hubbell, Lawyers.com, and Internet Brand's Nolo legal division creating the largest online legal network. Although certain changes are being made and particularly towards Internet access, the joint venture will still operate under the name of Martindale-Hubbell. *Martindale-Hubbell Law Directory* and the *Law Digest* can be accessed through martindale.com and www.martindale.com/Products_and_Services/Law_Digest.aspx.

### [c]  Use

The initial volumes that comprise the directory are a helpful aid in locating attorneys. They also help law students to learn something about the law firms and attorneys before they begin job interviews. There are two volumes listing lawyers and firms in over 165 countries.

The law digest volume is a quick resource for determining the particular uniform laws of the states. It provides information about the uniform laws as well as the statutory provisions of the states through abstracts. In addition to its Law Digest volume, there is an International Law Digest. Although it is a helpful reference, the researcher should not rely on these abstracts as official or definitive information. As with case abstracts in the digest or other resources, the information should always be confirmed in the original text such as the code or reporter.

## [d]   Location Method

**EXAMPLE:** Your client made a will in Florida but died while residing in Texas. You need to know if Texas has the Uniform Anatomical Gift Act. Without checking the Texas Code provisions, how could you answer this question?

### [i]      Print Version

This problem could be resolved by using the *Martindale-Hubbell Law Directory*. In the print version, the researcher should locate the last volume of *Martindale-Hubbell* which is the law digest volume. In that volume, find the section for Texas. Then check the appropriate subject heading which would be under Estates and Trusts with a subheading of the Uniform Anatomical Gift Act. Read the provision and cite to the Texas Code provision itself and not to *Martindale-Hubbell* which is a secondary source.

### [ii]      Electronic Version

Directory information can be found through the electronic versions. *Martindale Hubbell Law Directory* can be accessed through Lexis Advance. WestlawNext provides directory information through its FindLaw Lawyer Directory. In the example concerning the Uniform Anatomical Gift Act, the researcher could use Lexis Advance to locate the *Law Digest* of *Martindale-Hubbell Law Directory* and to determine if Texas has the Uniform Anatomical Gift Act. The researcher would find that Texas has adopted the Act. The provision leads to various sections of the Health and Safety Code and the Transportation Code.

### [iii]      Internet Version

On the Internet, *Martindale-Hubbell* may be accessed through www.lawyers.com. There are a number of other Internet sites such as FindLaw at www.findlaw.com and Legalserv at www.hg.org/attorney.html which provide directory information.

### MARTINDALE-HUBBELL CHECKLIST

**Print Version**

1. Locate the last volume of *Martindale-Hubbell* which is the law digest volume. Currently, the print volumes exist, but things may change with the 2014 joint venture.

2. Find the section for Texas.

3. Look under the appropriate subject headings. In this case, it would be under Estates and Trusts with a subheading of the Uniform Anatomical Gift Act.

4. If further use of the provision or analysis is necessary, then obtain the Texas Code cite.

5. Read the provision and cite from the Texas Code itself and not from any information from *Martindale-Hubbell*.

**Electronic Version**

1. Using Lexis Advance, the researcher can access the *Law Digest* of *Martindale-Hubbell Law Directory*. On Lexis Advance, however, LexisNexis indicates that the *Law Digest* is current through 2010 and that it is no longer being updated. These materials have been archived.

2. Through Profiler on WestlawNext, the researcher can find profiles of attorneys and judges from all 50 states, Puerto Rico, the Virgin Islands, the District of Columbia, Canada, England, and Europe.

**Internet Version**

1. Both *Martindale-Hubbell Law Directory* and the *Law Digest* can also be found on martindale.com. The LexisNexis Store makes the *Law Digest* available for purchase on CD-ROM.

2. Various sites on the Internet such as FindLaw and Legalserv provide directory information.

## C.  ADDITIONAL TIPS

1. Secondary sources are helpful research aids, however, the primary authority must always be found and read.

2. In addition, the primary source must always be updated. For example, an attorney used information from a prior brief but failed to check, read, and update the information. The statute had in fact been amended which could have easily been found if the proper research process had been followed. This is gross negligence. Ironically, the amendment was actually more favorable to the client's position than the original provision. There are examples in the reporters of where an attorney is reprimanded by the court for failing to cite the current provision.

3. Be sure to read the information to insure that it is relevant for the client. This is particularly true with form books where the form needs to be carefully and thoroughly read and modified if necessary.

# Chapter 10

# FOREIGN AND INTERNATIONAL RESEARCH

## A. OVERVIEW

Generally, foreign and international legal research is not taught in the first year legal research class. Therefore, the discussion in this chapter will be a brief overview simply to raise awareness that there are both different legal systems as well as international law that may affect doing business in a foreign country. As world trade and international dealings continue to increase, there is a greater demand to understand the legal ramifications of transactions and conduct in foreign countries.

Several terms should be defined:

- Foreign law is the domestic law of another country except it is not domestic law of the United States.

- International law is the law between or among countries.

- Comparative law is the comparison of the law or legal systems of different countries around the world. This study examines the similarities and differences between countries or legal systems. It is not the law itself but a method or approach for studying the law.

First year students are usually surprised to know that most other countries do not share the same kind of legal system as the United States. There are three major legal systems — the common law tradition, the civil law tradition, and the socialist law tradition. The common law tradition has its roots in England during the Middle Ages and was applied around the world in the British colonies. For example, Great Britain, Australia, New Zealand, Canada, India, and the United States are common law countries. The civil law system has its roots in Roman law and spread throughout Europe with the Roman Empire. Countries such as France, Germany, Austria, Switzerland, Italy, Spain, Mexico, and Japan are examples of civil law countries. The socialist legal tradition has its roots in Soviet law. For example, Russia, China, Cuba, and North Korea are within the socialist legal tradition.

The researcher may encounter certain problems when researching the law of another country. For example:

- Language could be a problem because the laws of foreign countries are written in the official language of the country. Even if a researcher speaks the language of the country, conversational language and legal language can be different. There may be issues of having the information translated into English, and therefore, translation issues may arise.

- Beyond the language issue, the litigation process and procedures may be different than in the United States. Thus, it takes an understanding of the legal process and procedures.

- Publication of legal materials may be an issue. Access to foreign law will be very different among the three major legal systems. The government of a particular country may or may not publish all of their legal materials. Even if they do, it may be slow and out of date.

The weight of authority is different between the common law countries and the civil and socialist law countries. In common law countries, there is greater emphasis on and authority of case law. This is not true in civil law and socialist law countries which give greater emphasis to a code. The publication of information may also be different in civil and socialist law countries. Assuming there is a successful plaintiff, damages will be an issue and particularly punitive damages. Procedural issues such enforcement of judgments may be a consideration. For example, will a foreign country enforce a United States judgment that includes punitive damages?

With this brief overview in mind, the remainder of this chapter will provide an outline of basic sources and strategies to begin foreign and international law research.

## B.  FOREIGN LAW

### [1]  Finding Materials in Print, Electronic, and Internet Versions

As a general proposition, common law countries have a written or unwritten constitution, legislation, regulations, and one or more levels of a court structure to decide cases. As indicated above, one of the distinguishing characteristics of these countries is the importance and weight of case law. In a common law system, the court will review, interpret, and apply the laws of a state or country.

In civil law or socialist law countries, there are a constitution, a code and/or statutes, and case law. But the key difference is the emphasis on case law. Case law is significantly less important in interpreting and applying the law to the case than in common law countries. Unlike the United States and other common law countries, scholarly writings are more influential and authoritative than the weight that secondary authority is given in a common law country.

The following steps should be followed when researching foreign law. First, the researcher needs to determine whether the country is a common law, civil law, or socialist law country. Beginning with the legal tradition will help to explain the type of legal materials that are available and the relative weight of authority. Brill's *Foreign Law Guide* provides an introductory overview of the legal system and legal history of approximately 190 countries and is available in print and online. JuriGlobe's *World Legal Systems* is another online source that is a quick reference for countries. The CIA produces the *World Factbook* which provides information on the history, people, government, economy, geography, communications, transportation, military, and transnational issues for 267 world entities. The *World Factbook* is available at https://www.cia.gov/library/publications/the-world-factbook/. *Modern Legal System Cyclopedia* is multi-volume set that discusses the legal system of countries but is somewhat dated. *Legal Systems of the World* is a four volume set that is edited by Herbert Kritzer and organized by specific jurisdictions.

There are other online sources. For example, Findlaw provides links to foreign law sources at http://www.findlaw.com/12international/countries/index.html. LLRX has comparative and foreign law at http://www.llrx.com/comparative_and_foreign_law. html. In addition, librarians at various law schools have compiled guides to foreign law. For example, Columbia Law School has *A Selective List of Guides to Foreign Legal Research*, available at http://library.law.columbia.edu/guides/A_Selective_List_of_ Guides_to_Foreign_Legal_Research; Duke Law School has foreign and comparative law at http://www.law.duke.edu/lib/researchguides/foreign; or Yale Law School has a *Country-by-Country Guide to Foreign Law Research* at http://library.law.yale.edu/ research/guides/country-guide. These guides connect the researcher to the best research guides and databases for each country. The Library of Congress in its foreign and international law section has foreign law guides for select countries at http://www. loc.gov/law/help/foreign.php. They include an introduction to the legal system, official sources of law, print, and web resources.

Second, determine what type of problem it is. Will the answer to the problem be located in the constitution, code, case law, or secondary authority? A source such as Brill's *Foreign Law Guide* provides an outline of the judicial and legislative system; primary and secondary sources of law and legal information; links to major online sources; and identifies major legal publications. For example, if this is a constitutional law problem, the constitution of countries can be found in the multi-volume set entitled *Constitutions of the Countries of the World* which is edited by A.P. Blaustein and G.H. Flanz. There are also online sources such as *Constitution Finder* at http://confinder. richmond.cdu/ or Hcin Online has current and historical constitutions.

If this is a statutory or case law problem, Lexis Advance and WestlawNext have these materials for some foreign countries and the European Union. WestlawNext also provides databases for foreign countries and the European Union.

Global Courts is a website that will lead the researcher to Supreme Court decisions from 129 foreign countries or at least a way to find those decisions. This information is available at http://www.globalcourts.com/. Websites such LEXADIN: *The World Law Guide* links to full texts of codes and legislation for foreign countries, but the information is in the language of the country. GlobaLex also provides country guides to foreign legal materials that are written by legal research experts. The guides will lead the researcher to sources that are available in print and online.

Finding secondary authority can be challenging. WestlawNext and Lexis Advance have some foreign treatises and journals. The databases of law review articles are primarily for journals in the United States. They are a means, however, for finding citations to foreign laws, cases, and other documents. In particular, articles can be a good source for comparative law studies. Likewise, the *Index to Legal Periodicals* (ILP) and *LegalTrac* are indices that can lead to articles that provide comparisons with foreign laws and legal systems. These indices are available in print and online. The *Index to Foreign Legal Periodicals* (IFLP) can be found in larger law libraries, but most periodicals that are indexed are in languages other than English, but many articles have English abstracts.

It may become necessary to hire local counsel. *Martindale-Hubbell International Law Directory* is a two volume annual directory. It is both in print and online and allows the researcher to search for lawyers by region, country, and city in 160 countries. It also has a separate biographical entry for many firms. *Martindale-Hubbell International Law Digest* has summaries of foreign law and the text of many international treaties. It is no longer published in print, but it is available on LexisNexis. *Chambers Global: The World's Leading Lawyers* is also an annual directory of lawyers in 185 countries and is available at http://www.chambersandpartners.com/. The researcher can search by an individual attorney's name, the law firm name, and the country. On the websites of U.S. embassies and consulates, there is a list of American lawyers who are licensed to practice in the foreign country and who are willing to assist U.S. clients. The lists include the following information for the lawyer: name, contact information, educational background, areas of specialization, and the languages spoken by the lawyer.

---

### CHECKLIST FOR FOREIGN LAW

1. Learn background information on the foreign country's legal system including the types and weight of primary and secondary sources.

2. Determine what type of problem that it is.

   a. Check any primary sources that may be available in print, electronic, or Internet versions.

   b. Check for any secondary sources that may be available in print, electronic, or Internet versions.

3. Determine whether local counsel is necessary.

---

## C. ADDITIONAL TIPS

1. For information on countries of the world, check the Library of Congress' *Guide to Law Online* at http://www.loc.gov/law/help/guide/nations.php which lists countries. When selecting a country, the site will give the research legal information such as the Constitution, Executive, Judicial, Legislative, and general resources such as legal guides.

2. The Law Library of Congress has prepared guides for a selection of countries which includes an introduction to the legal system, official sources of law, resources in print and Internet at http://www.loc.gov/law/help/foreign.php.

3. The Department of State has some helpful tips on dealing with foreign lawyers which is available at http://travel.state.gov/content/travel/english/legal-considerations/judicial/retaining-a-foreign-attorney.html.

4. Hieros Gamos also has tools for researching foreign and international law at http://www.hg.org/1table.html. Under the "law" tab, the researcher can click on "law worldwide," and get information on foreign countries, the United Nations, or the European Union.

5. GlobaLex has research guides for foreign, international, and comparative law research at http://www.law.nyu.edu/global/researchtools.

6. Findlaw also has a foreign and international section at http://www.findlaw.com/12international/index.html. It has listings for countries, the Constitutions of the World, and U.S. Embassy information for embassies around the world.

7. If it is necessary to hire local counsel, determine what type of lawyer you need. For example, in England there are barristers who represent clients in court and solicitors who help prepare a case or do more transactional type of work. Notaries in foreign countries are different than in the United States. In civil law countries, notaries can draft certain documents and help administer and settle estates.

8. Be aware that few countries publish legal information as thoroughly or accessibly as the United States.

9. Although a researcher can be confident in finding the law in the United States through the pattern and practice described in the previous chapters, it is unlikely that the researcher will have the same confidence in researching foreign law.

10. At times, researching foreign law can be time-consuming and frustrating, but things are getting better in the electronic and digital age.

11. Google Translate may help with language issues. Be careful when it comes to legal words and terms.

## D.   INTERNATIONAL LAW

As mentioned above, international law is the law between or among countries. International law can be between neighboring countries such as the North American Free Trade Agreement (NAFTA) which was entered into on January 1, 1994 between the United States, Canada, and Mexico. It can also be with complex intergovernmental organizations such as the United Nations or the European Union.

International law is not new as it has existed since the mid-19th century. But, it was in the 20th century after the two World Wars and the formation of the League of Nations that international law blossomed and the foundations of modern public international law developed. Ultimately, the League of Nations was replaced by the United Nations which was founded under the UN Charter. The United Nations has a vast organizational structure and body of law which is beyond the scope of this chapter.

International law is divided into two parts:

- Public international law concerns the structure and conduct of sovereign nation states. For example, intergovernmental organizations such as the United Nations.

- Private international law concerns conflicts between private persons instead of states. In civil law jurisdictions, it is distinguished from public international law and is analogous to conflict of law issues in the United States. With expanding international trade, private international law can be a concern for individuals and corporations.

This section will focus on public international law and suggest some sources of law and methods of finding it. Specifically, this section will outline treaties and international agreements from a United States perspective and where they can be found.

Traditional sources of international law are treaties, custom, general principles of law, judicial decisions, and teachings of publicists. Many scholars opine that Article 38.1 of the Statute of the International Court of Justice suggests a hierarchy of sources in its sequential arrangement with treaties, international customs, and general principles as the three primary sources. The provision, however, simply states that the Court "shall apply" these sources of international law. Judicial decisions and teachings of highly qualified publicists (scholarly writings) are expressly designated as the "subsidiary" sources of international law. Each source of law will be discussed.

## [1] Treaties

A treaty is simply a formal agreement between two or more countries. Treaties can be on a variety of topics such as peace agreements or trade agreements. Treaties may be bilateral as between two countries or they can be multilateral if entered into by three or more countries. Treaties are the most important single source of international law.

The United States Constitution has several provisions for treaties which describe the role of the branches of government and the authority of the treaty. For example:

- Article I, Section 8 grants Congress power to regulate commerce among foreign nations;

- Article I, Section 10 prohibits the individual states of the United States from entering into a treaty;

- Article II, Section 2 gives the President the power to make treaties with the advice and consent of the Senate if two thirds of the Senators present concur;

- Article III, Section 2 gives jurisdiction over treaties made to resolve disputes involving international parties; and

- Article IV states that treaties of the United States become the supreme law of the land.

When a nation wants to become a party or signatory to a treaty, it goes through the process for approving a treaty such as the one discussed above for the United States.

Once a nation becomes a signatory to a treaty, it will become necessary for that nation to change its domestic law to fulfill the requirements of the treaty. This is called implementing legislation. Just as it is important for research purposes to know of the terms of the treaty, it is also important to know the implementing legislation.

Multilateral treaties and particularly those which the United States is a signatory are generally more readily available. Treaties can be found in both print and online versions. They are also in official and unofficial sources. As the researcher has learned in other chapters of the text, official sources are slow and can take years to publish. Official sources include the *United States Code*; *Treaties and Other International Acts Series (T.I.A.S.)*; and *United States Treaties (U.S.T.)*. Hein Online has both *T.I.A.S.* and *U.S.T.* The Department of State has *T.I.A.S.* and the Library of Congress also has a searchable database in its Thomas treaties page available at thomas.loc. gov/home/treaties/treaties.html. Both Lexis Advance and WestlawNext have treaties databases and particularly for the European Union.

The researcher needs to check the status of the treaty. The Department of State publishes *Treaties in Force* on an annual basis. It is available in print version, electronic versions such as on Lexis Advance, and on the Internet through Hein Online. The print version is divided into two sections. Section 1 has bilateral treaties that are listed by country and subject headings. Section 2 has multilateral treaties which are arranged by subject matter. The Department of State also has on its website Treaty Actions at http://www.state.gov/s/l/treaty/c3428.htm, but the researcher would have to search by date.

Because the United States Senate must give advice and consent, information can be found on its website at http://www.senate.gov/pagelayout/legislative/d_three_sections_ with_teasers/treaties.htm. The "Treaties Received" section identifies treaties that were received from the President during the current Congress or any committee referral actions that were taken. The "Treaties Approved" section identifies treaties that were approved by the Senate during the current Congress and links to the treaty ratification resolutions.

*CCH Congressional Index* is a two-volume looseleaf service that is issued for each congressional session. The volume for the Senate contains a section on treaties that are pending before the Senate and provides its status. This is a good source if the researcher is searching for pre-ratification treaty information.

Treaties in the *United States Code* or the unofficial versions of the *United States Code Annotated* or *United States Code Service* can be updated through *Shepard's U.S. Citations* in print or on Lexis Advance or KeyCite on WestlawNext.

The researcher can also find any interpretations of the treaty or legislative intent. For example, Senate hearings usually by the Senate Foreign Relations Committee can provide a wealth of information. They can be found in print with *CIS Annual* or on Lexis Advance and WestlawNext. Another avenue may be the *United States Code Service* which is the annotated code and may provide case annotations for bilateral or multilateral treaties if the courts have interpreted the treaties.

When the United States is not a signatory to a treaty, it is more difficult to identify and locate them. This is particularly true if they are bilateral treaties. Multilateral treaties are generally done through either regional or international organizations such as the United Nations, European Union, or the World Trade Organization. Therefore, it is more efficient to check their websites. Secondary sources will enable the researcher to search for treaties by subject matter. For example, if the researcher wanted to know about the treaties concerning aviation, the researcher could go to a three-volume looseleaf service by Oceana entitled *Air and Aviation Treaties of the World*.

Hein Online has developed an extensive collection of treaties entitled the World Treaty Library. It covers treaties from 1648 to present for a total of more than 180,000 treaty records. There is an in-depth index of all the treaties which can be found through keyword, country, treaty number, treaty type, party, and subject. This is a major tool in finding treaties.

---

### CHECKLIST FOR TREATIES

1. The following are questions that the researcher should ask concerning any treaty:

    a. Has the United States or another country relevant to the problem entered into a treaty?

    b. Is the treaty still in force?

    c. Does the implementing legislation that was passed by the legislature exist?

    d. How do the terms of the treaty apply to the researcher's specific problem?

2. Locate the text of the treaty in either print, electronic, or Internet versions.

3. Determine the status of the treaty. For example, who are the signatories and when did it get ratified? Were there any reservations and declarations?

4. Locate implementing legislation.

5. Locate case law and commentary by experts.

6. Locate administering documents.

7. Locate legislative history or other background materials that would give the researcher insight on the meaning or application of the treaty.

8. Verify that the treaty is still in force.

---

## [2]   International Customs

Article 38.1 of the Statute of the International Court of Justice lists international customs as a source of international law. There are two requirements for customary law — state practice and acceptance of the practice. The role of custom in a civil law country has changed over time and with the particular country. For example, the French and the Germans tend to give different weight to custom.

As a practical matter, however, legislation often looks to custom for greater understanding of the legislation. For example, there may be a need for custom to explain whether a certain mark constitutes a signature. Having said that, the role of custom has diminished with the advancement and emphasis on codification. But one cannot deny the importance of custom in the development of the law.

From an American perspective, the *Restatement of the Law, Third, Foreign Relations Law of the United States* § 102 recognizes customary law as a source of law and is based on Article 38.1 of the Statute of the International Court of Justice. *Restatement* § 103 discusses pronouncements and comments: "Thus, for customary law the 'best evidence' is the proof of state practice, ordinarily by reference to official documents and other indications of governmental action."

Ian Brownlie in *Principles of Public International Law* lists the following sources as evidence of custom:

> The material sources of custom are very numerous and include the following: diplomatic correspondence, policy statements, press releases, the opinions of official legal advisers, official manuals on legal questions, e.g. manuals of military law, executive decisions and practices, orders to naval forces etc., comments by governments on drafts produced by the International Law Commission, state legislation, international and national judicial decisions, recitals in treaties and other international instruments, a pattern of treaties in the same form, the practice of international organs, and resolutions relating to legal questions in the United Nations General Assembly.

The United States Department of State publications include pronouncements that state the rules of international law and therefore are excellent resources for the evidence of custom. Examples of these documents include memorandums, letters from legal advisors, U.S. briefs, position papers, and remarks. The Department of State and the Office of the Legal Advisor provide many of these resources on their websites. In addition, the Department of State publishes the *Digest of United States Practice in International Law*. The *Digest* is an excellent source for information on the views and practice of the government concerning public and private intentional law.

There are also a variety of secondary authority in civil law countries that would articulate and analyze international custom. For example, Article 38 lists the writings of highly qualified publicists as a source. These writings can be found in treatises, periodicals, yearbooks, or digests. In civil law countries, yearbooks are published. *Yearbooks* are unofficial sources that are often published by a national law society. They include articles about international law and state practice, citations to official documents, and sometimes they include indexes, the full-text documents, and bibliographies of books and articles.

The researcher may also find references to custom in primary authority. In 1950, the International Law Commission of the United Nations listed treaties, decisions of national courts and international tribunals, national legislation as evidence of customary international law. *See* "Report of the International Law Commission to the General Assembly (Part II): Ways and Means of Making the Evidence of Customary International Law More Readily Available," [1950] 2 *Y.B. Int'l L. Comm'n* 367, ILC Doc. A/1316).

---

### CHECKLIST FOR INTERNATIONAL CUSTOM

1. Recognize that international custom is a source of law if it meets the traditional requirements of state practice and acceptance of the practice.

2. Find international custom through primary authority sources such as treaties, decisions of national courts and international tribunals, and national legislation.

3. Find international custom through secondary authority sources such as highly qualified publicists and yearbooks.

4. In the United States, check the United States Department of State website for documents and digests which would provide evidence of custom.

---

## [3]   General Principles of Law

General principles are those principles that apply in all major legal systems. For example, it is a general principle of law that persons who intentionally harm others should have to pay compensation or make reparation. General principles are derived from "norms of positive law or from the existence of the legal order itself . . . ." *See* Mary Ann Glendon, et al., *Comparative Legal Traditions* 204 (2d ed. 1994).

In most civil codes, there is a statement that where express law is absent, judges can use general principles to resolve disputes. "When there is no provision in an international treaty or statute nor any recognized customary principle of international law available for application in an international dispute, the general principles of law can be used to 'fill the gap.' " *See* James G. Apple, "What are General Principles of International Law?" available at http://www.judicialmonitor.org/archive_0707/generalprinciples.html.

The *Restatement of the Law (Third), the Foreign Relations of the United States* Section 102(4) states that "General principles common to the major legal systems, even if not incorporated or reflected in customary law or international agreement, may be invoked as supplementary rules of international law where appropriate." The comments state:

> General principles common to systems of national law may be resorted to as an independent source of law. That source of law may be important when there

has not been practice by states sufficient to give the particular principle status as customary law and the principle has not been legislated by general international agreement.

Other rules of law have been drawn from general principles. The *Restatement* gives examples such as rules relating to the administration of justice; *res judicata*; and rules of fair procedure generally. The *Restatement* also states that general principles may provide "rules of reason" such as the doctrine of estoppel, the principle that rights must not be abused, and the obligation to repair a wrong.

General principles can be obtained from both primary and secondary sources. Primary sources may include the domestic law of a country such as the domestic constitution, legislation, regulations, and case law. For example, the European Court of Justice has developed unwritten rules which are not expressly provided for in treaties, but they affect how European Union law is interpreted and applied. These principles may come from public international law or legal doctrines from member states or from the European Court of Human Rights. The general principles that are accepted under European Union Law include such things as fundamental human rights, proportionality, legal certainty, equality before the law, and subsidiarity. Secondary sources include, for example, the writings of publicists.

---

### CHECKLIST FOR GENERAL PRINCIPLES

1. Determine from where the general principles are derived.

2. Consider how general principles can be used to "fill the gap."

3. Consider whether general principles can be obtained from both primary and secondary authority.

---

## [4] Judicial Opinions

The Statute of the International Court of Justice § 38.1 states that judicial decisions are a "subsidiary" means for determining the rules of law. In addition, Article 59 states that International Court of Justice (ICJ) decisions have "no binding force except between the parties and in respect of that particular case." These statements are a dramatic difference from the common law perspective of the role and authority of judicial opinions.

Section 103 of the *Restatement of the Law (Third) of Foreign Relations Law of the United States* defines judicial decisions as "evidence" of international law. Comment b to Section 103 recognizes that an ICJ decision "has no binding force except between the parties and in respect of that particular case," but suggests that the ICJ and other permanent international courts in fact pay considerable attention to past decisions.

Decisions from the permanent international courts can be found on the Internet. Some examples are:

- The International Court of Justice at www.icj-cij.org/;

- The Permanent Court of International Justice (League of Nations) at http://www.worldcourts.com/pcij/eng/;

- The European Court of Human Rights at http://www.echr.coe.int/;

- The Inter-American Court of Human Rights at http://www.corteidh.or.cr/;

- International Criminal Court at http://www.icc-cpi.int/ and http://www.un.org/icc/.

In addition, there may be decisions of national courts that pertain to international issues. It is interesting that neither the Statute of the International Court of Justice nor the *Restatement of Foreign Relations Law of the United States* state that national court decisions on matters of international law cannot be considered. There are both print and electronic versions of these decisions. For example:

- *International Law Reports* are cases from national jurisdictions and international tribunals and courts. They are available in print and electronic versions.

- *American International Law Cases* is a print series that contains decisions of federal and state courts of the United States on questions of public international law.

In the United States, there are other ways of finding cases on international issues including:

- Digests such as the *United States Supreme Court Digest* and *West's Federal Practice Digest.*

- *American Law Reports (A.L.R.).*

- Electronic databases on Lexis Advance and WestlawNext.

The researcher can also check secondary authority in the United States. Treatises or law journal articles may be helpful in explaining the legal system, court decision, or the ramifications of the case on a particular issue. Secondary authority may also be a tool for finding a case or other primary authority relevant to the problem.

The researcher should also be aware that decisions in civil law jurisdictions tend to be much shorter than in the United States. Because the case has no precedential value, as a general rule, there is no need to have detailed opinions and analysis. Opinions may be two or three pages long. One or more judges can also write separate or dissenting opinions.

Another difference is that courts such as the International Court of Justice (ICJ) can issue advisory opinions. These advisory opinions, which are called advisory proceedings, are on legal questions referred to it by duly authorized United Nations organs and specialized agencies. Courts in the United States do not issue advisory opinions.

ICJ opinions are in both print and electronic versions. In print, they are first issued as separate documents and then printed in two series. The *ICJ Reports* contain reports of judgments, advisory opinions, and orders. They are cited as *ICJ Reports* with the year. They are published and indexed in both English and French. The second series is the *ICJ Pleadings*. This series contains pleadings, oral arguments, and documents produced by the parties and listed in chronological order. This series is cited as *ICJ Pleadings* and have the case name and volume. These documents are also printed in English and French. The ICJ website has materials listed by case.

---

### CHECKLIST OF JUDICIAL DECISIONS

1. Recognize that there are major differences on the weight and authority of judicial decisions in common law and civil law jurisdictions. In civil law countries, court decisions only have binding effect on the parties in that particular case.

2. For the various international courts, check the court's website.

3. For cases in the United States on international issues, check traditional finding methods such as the digests, *A.L.R.*, Lexis Advance, and West-lawNext.

4. For cases that were found through U.S. finding methods, be sure to update them through *Shepard's* in print or on Lexis Advance or KeyCite for WestlawNext.

5. Determine whether there are treatises or law journal articles that would explain the legal system, court decision, or the ramifications of the case on a particular issue.

---

## [5]  Teachings of Publicists

The Statute of the International Court of Justice § 38.1 states: "the teachings of the most highly qualified publicists of the various nations, as subsidiary means for the determination of rules of law." Section 103 of the *Restatement of the Law (Third) of Foreign Relations Law of the United States* phrases it slightly differently. It states that "substantial weight is accorded to . . . (c) the writings of scholars."

As with scholarly writings in the United States, what weight the judges give the writing will depend on several factors including the reputation of the author, whether this is an isolated view, whether the view represents a consensus of respected writers. The *Restatement* states it like this: "Which publicists are 'the most highly qualified' is, of course, not susceptible of conclusive proof, and the authority of writings as evidence of international law differs greatly. The views of the International Law Commission have sometimes been considered especially authoritative."

The reporter's notes to the *Restatement* state that these writings ". . . include treatises and other writings of authors of standing; resolutions of scholarly bodies such as the Institute of International Law (Institut de droit international) and the International Law Association; draft texts and reports of the International Law Commission, and systematic scholarly presentations of international law such as this *Restatement*." Thus, the researcher can find them in general or specialized treatises, commentaries on the codes, monographs, law review articles, case notes, and any expert opinions in connection with the litigation.

---

### CHECKLIST FOR TEACHING OF PUBLICISTS

1. Recognize that the writings of publicists are given greater weight than in the United States.

2. Evaluate the strength of the writing including the reputation of the author, whether this is an isolated view, whether the view represents a consensus of respected writers.

3. Find scholarly writings in general or specialized treatises, commentaries on the codes, monographs, law review articles, case notes, and any expert opinions in connection with the litigation.

---

## E. ADDITIONAL TIPS

1. Check the websites for major international organizations such as the United Nations and the European Union websites. There is a wealth of information on these sites.

2. A popular website for legal research is the Library of Congress' *Guide to Law Online* at http://www.loc.gov/law/help/guide.php.

3. The Law Library of Congress has a resource, which is in the progress of being updated, called Global Legal Information Network (GLIN) at http://www.glin.gov.com. This database has laws, judicial opinions and regulations for foreign countries and international organization.

4. Hieros Gamos also has tools for researching foreign and international law at http://www.hg.org/1table.html. Under the "law" tab, the researcher can click on "law worldwide," and get information on foreign countries, the United Nations, or the European Union.

5. GlobaLex has research guides for foreign, international, and comparative law research at http://www.law.nyu.edu/global/researchtools.

6. Justia provides sources that the researcher can use to search law in Mexico, South America, Central America, and the Caribbean at https://www.justia.com/.

7. There are numerous academic websites that provide resources for international law. For example, these include Columbia Law School's site at http://library.law.columbia.edu/guides/Researching_Public_International_Law; Yale Law Library: *Country by Country Guide to Foreign Law Resources* at http://library.law.yale.edu/research/guides/country-guide (links to both free and fee-based resources); and Washburn University School of Law site at http://www.washlaw.edu/forint/index.html provides foreign and international law resources.

8. Findlaw also has an international section with information on the United

Nations and other international organizations and topics http://www.findlaw.com/12international/index.html.

9. Recently, *A.L.R.* started a new series to meet the demands of international practice. It is called *A.L.R. International.* There is an analysis of legal issues and case law from both English and non-English speaking countries such as Brazil, Russia, India, China, and Korea. The topics that are covered in this set are those arising under international conventions and treaties. Effective January 2010, *A.L.R. International* is also available online.

# Appendix

# SAMPLE RESEARCH PROBLEMS

## PROBLEM I

### FACTS

Tulip, a mixed-breed dog, escaped its yard in Anyville, Texas, and was promptly collected by local animal control. The distraught family went to retrieve the dog but had insufficient funds to secure its release. The shelter placed a "hold for owner" tag on the dog's pen, but when the family returned, the shelter had mistakenly put the dog down. Devastated, the family seeks emotional damages for the dog's loss.

The family consults your law firm to determine whether there is a cause of action for loss of companionship for a pet's wrongful death.

### RESEARCH ASSIGNMENT

Describe the nature of the authority you seek and the reason(s) you have selected that authority. Next, discuss the most efficient research tools which you will select to find, update, and verify the authority. To the extent possible, integrate print and electronic sources.

### OUTLINE OF THE SUGGESTED RESEARCH PROCESS

The authority appropriate to this problem is primary mandatory authority in the form of Texas case law found in Texas appellate decisions through the steps described below.

Analyze the facts according to the TAPP rule.

## [A]   Print Version

1.  Find the appropriate case law in the *Texas Digest, Second Series* by using:

    a.  Descriptive Word Method: Use key words and phrases, such as "negligence" and "animals" in the Descriptive Word Index and pocket part, if any, to identify appropriate topic and key numbers; or

    b.  Topic Method: Go to the digest volume and pocket part covering the relevant issue, and examine the topic "Analysis," which is like a table of contents of the topic and key number subjects. Select the most appropriate key number(s).

2.  Read the case summaries below the relevant key number(s) and get cites to cases closest in their facts to the client's problem.

3.  Locate and read the case(s) in the appropriate *Southwestern Reporter* volume(s), advance sheets, or the Texas Supreme Court Journal.

4.  Update in *Shepard's Texas Citations* or case volumes.

5.  If you can locate no primary mandatory authority, consult primary persuasive or secondary authority.

    a.  Primary persuasive authority — use American Digest with key words and phrases described in 2(a) to locate decisions from other jurisdictions.

    b.  Update through state *Shepard's* print volumes.

    c.  Consult and update relevant secondary sources, such as *A.L.R.* or the *Restatement of the Law (Torts)*.

## [B]  Electronic Version

1.  Analyze the facts according to the TAPP rule with the key words and phrases identified above in Lexis Advance or WestlawNext Texas cases.

2.  Find any appropriate decisions and update through *Shepard's* on Lexis Advance or KeyCite on WestlawNext.

3.  If you can find no primary mandatory authority, consult primary persuasive authority by expanding to all state cases or secondary authority, such as *A.L.R.* or the *Restatement of the Law (Torts)* through Lexis Advance or WestlawNext, which provides full coverage of the *A.L.R.*

## [C]  Internet Version

1.  Texas state court decisions are accessible at specific websites, such as supreme.courts.state.tx.us for Texas Supreme Court decisions and txcourts. gov for Texas Courts of Appeals decisions.

2.  Fastcase provides coverage of Texas decisions, as well as Bad Law Bot to flag cases with negative history. Casemaker also offers coverage of Texas state decisions with Casecheck+ to determine whether the case is still good law and Subsequent History for writ or petition histories of cases.

# PROBLEM II

## FACTS

A non-profit humanist group wishes to solemnize its members' marriages, but it lacks capacity to do so under Indiana's statute that does not recognize humanist leaders as "clergy," and imposes criminal penalties for others who perform marriages. The group consults your law firm to challenge the Indiana statute for violating the First Amendment to the U.S. Constitution.

## RESEARCH ASSIGNMENT

Identify the nature of the authority you seek and the reason(s) you have selected that authority. Next, discuss the appropriate research tool(s) which are necessary to find, update, and verify the authority. To the extent possible, integrate print and electronic processes.

## OUTLINE OF THE SUGGESTED RESEARCH PROCESS

The authority appropriate to this problem is primary mandatory authority in the form of an Indiana statute and any interpretive decisions. This authority is located in the annotated state statutes using the following steps.

Analyze the facts according to the TAPP rule.

## [A]  Print Version

1. Find the provision through any of the following methods:

    a. Popular Name Method: Use the popular name table in the Annotated Indiana Statutes General Index if you have a popular name;

    b. Topic Method: Go to the individual subject index if you already know which code contains the provision; or

    c. Descriptive Word Method: Go to the General Subject Index of the Indiana statutes to look under "marriage solemnization" to locate statute labeled "Persons authorized to solemnize marriage."

2. Read the provision in the Annotated Indiana Statutes. Note the language regarding the effectiveness date of the legislation.

3. Update the statute by:

    a. The annual pocket part, unless the code is paperbound;

    b. Any pamphlet supplements;

    c. *Session Law Service*;

    d. Update with *Shepard's Indiana Citations*, statutes volumes.

4. Find interpretive cases, if any, by:

    a. *Index of Decisions* following the text of the statute;

    b. The appropriate Note of Decision number(s) in bound volume or paper pamphlet, along with the case citation.

5. Update the cases by:

    a.  The annual pocket part, unless the code is paperbound;

    b.  Any pamphlet supplements (semi-annual);

    c.  The advance sheets of the relevant reporter;

    d.  *Shepard's Indiana Citations* cases volumes.

## [B]  Electronic Version

1. Analyze the facts according to the TAPP rule with the Popular Name, Topic, or Descriptive Word Method described above on Lexis Advance or West-lawNext.

2. Find relevant statutory provisions, note currency, and any interpretive decisions and update through *Shepard's* on Lexis Advance or KeyCite on WestlawNext.

## [C]  Internet Version

1. Fastcase provides coverage of Indiana statutes in its state law libraries. Note currency dates. Check for interpretive decisions and update with Bad Law Bot.

2. Casemaker covers Indiana statutes in its state law libraries. Note currency dates and consult Statute Annotator for how the courts have interpreted the statute. Update any relevant decision with Casecheck+.

# PROBLEM III

## FACTS

Your client worked for a package delivery company as a driver when she became pregnant. Prohibited by her doctor from lifting over 20 pounds, she sought accommodation similar to that received by other employees injured on the job. When the employer refused her accommodation request, the client sought protection of the Pregnancy Discrimination Act.

## RESEARCH ASSIGNMENT

Describe thoroughly the authority you seek and the reasons you have selected that authority. Discuss the relevant research tools necessary to find, update, and verify the authority. To the extent possible, integrate print and electronic processes.

## OUTLINE OF THE SUGGESTED RESEARCH PROCESS

The authority appropriate for this problem is primary mandatory authority in the form of federal legislation, any relevant legislative history and interpretive case law.

Analyze the facts according to the TAPP rule.

## [A]  Print Version

1. Find the federal statutory provision using any of the following methods:

    a. Popular Name Method: Use the popular name table in the *U.S.C.S.* or *U.S.C.A.* General Index to get the cite to the Pregnancy Discrimination Act (PDA);

    b. Topic Method: Go to the individual subject index if you already know the statute is in the "Public Health and Welfare" Code, Title 42; or

    c. Descriptive Word Method: Go to the General Subject Index with the words that you isolated during the TAPP analysis.

2. Read the federal statute in the bound volume or pamphlet of the *U.S.C.S.* or *U.S.C.A.*. Note the public law number and any reference to a legislative history, such as a committee report. Be sure to verify the legislation's effectiveness date as well.

3. Update the statute by noting its most recent amendment, if any, in the bound volume historical note following the legislation's language:

    a. Check the annual *U.S.C.A.* or *U.S.C.S.* pocket part, unless the code is paperbound;

    b. Check pamphlet supplements;

    c. Check the unofficial session laws, such as *U.S.C.C.A.N.* or *U.S.C.S.* pamphlets; and then

    d. Update the statute in *Shepard's Federal Statutes Citations*, statutes volume.

4. Find interpretive cases:

    a. Check the bound volume Notes of Decision;

    b. Check the Notes of Decision in the pocket part, if any;

    c. Check the Notes of Decision in any supplementary pamphlet;

    d. Check the Cumulative Table of Statutes Construed in advance sheets of all federal court reporters; and

    e. Update any relevant cases in the appropriate *Shepard's* volumes.

## [B]　Electronic Version

1. Analyze the facts according to the TAPP rule. Use the Popular Name Method for the "Pregnancy Discrimination Act," the Topic Method, or the Descriptive Word Method to find the federal statute through *U.S.C.S.* on Lexis Advance or *U.S.C.A.* on WestlawNext.

2. Note the effectiveness date and legislative history references.

3. *U.S.C.S.* and *U.S.C.A.* maintain currency often within a month of the present date; be sure to check.

4. Find any interpretive decisions from the federal district, circuit, and/or U.S. Supreme Courts.

5. Update the statute and any interpretive decisions with *Shepard's* on Lexis Advance or KeyCite on WestlawNext.

## [C]　Internet Version

1. Federal statutes can be located with the methods described above through the U.S. Code's official website provided by the Office of Law Revision Council (OLRC) (uscode.house.gov) or FDsys (gpo.gov/fdsys/browse/collectionUSCode). These sources provide no access to interpretive opinions. If the researcher has a case citation, a specific federal court's website, such as supremecourt.gov, or federal circuit court opinions, uscourts.gov, may provide the full opinion, though there is no update service.

2. Fastcase and Casemaker provide access to federal statutes. Fastcase provides cases interpreting federal laws, updated through its Bad Law Bot feature, and Casemaker offers a similar service through its Statute Annotator.

## PROBLEM IV

### FACTS

Your client owns a factory with a generous sick leave policy. One of the employees was diagnosed with cancer and utilized the seven months of unpaid sick leave under the employer's plan. When the worker sought an extension, the company denied the request and terminated her when she did not return to work. The discharged worker brought suit, claiming that the employer did not notify her that twelve weeks of her absence would count as FMLA (Family and Medical Leave Act) leave, as required by federal regulations.

### RESEARCH ASSIGNMENT

Describe thoroughly the authority you seek and the reasons you have selected that authority. Discuss the relevant research necessary to find, update, and verify the authority. To the extent possible, integrate print and electronic processes.

### OUTLINE OF THE SUGGESTED RESEARCH PROCESS

The authority appropriate for this problem is primary mandatory authority in the form of federal regulations implementing the federal statute and any interpretive decisions addressing the regulations.

## [A]  Print Version

1.  Locate interpretive rules or regulations in the *Code of Federal Regulations (C.F.R.)* in print:

    a.  The Parallel Table of Authorities in the annual *C.F.R. General Index and Finding Aids* volume using the U.S. Code title and section number if you have it to cross reference the applicable *C.F.R.* title and part number.

    b.  Descriptive Word Method: Go to the annual paperbound *C.F.R. General Index and Finding Aids* volume with the words that you isolated during the TAPP analysis.

    c.  Topic Method: Go to the appropriate title in the *C.F.R.* if you know which of the 50 titles is applicable.

    d.  Agency Method: If you know which agency enforces the rules, consult the list in the annual *C.F.R. General Index and Finding Aids* for the title and part numbers.

2.  Read the regulation(s) and note the cite to the enabling legislation.

3.  Update the regulation(s) by:

    a.  The supplementary pamphlet: Check the monthly *C.F.R. List of Sections Affected*; and

    b.  The most recent daily *Federal Register* cumulative list of sections affected.

4.  Find interpretive cases by:

    a.  *Shepard's C.F.R. Citations*, which provides interpretive opinions for federal court decisions; or

    b.  Federal agency publications for any federal agency decisions.

5.  Update the judicial or agency decisions through *Shepard's* citations for the relevant federal reporter.

## [B]  Electronic Version

1.  Locate the relevant rule or regulation by using the methods described above through Lexis Advance or WestlawNext.

2.  Both services continually update the regulation current within a few days.

3.  Lexis Advance and WestlawNext provide citing references to interpretive cases.

4.  Selected agency decisions are available through Lexis Advance or WestlawNext.

5.  Update all judicial opinions through *Shepard's* on Lexis Advance or KeyCite on WestlawNext.

## [C]  Internet Version

1.  Locate the relevant rule or regulation through the methods described above using the FDsys e-CFR, updated within a couple of days.

2.  Fastcase and Casemaker provide access to the *C.F.R.*

3.  Locate interpretive agency opinions through the relevant agency website.

4.  Consult Fastcase or Casemaker coverage of selected agency opinions.

# INDEX

[References are to sections.]

## A

**ADMINISTRATIVE LAW**
Cities (See MUNICIPAL LEGISLATION)
Counties (See MUNICIPAL LEGISLATION)
Federal (See FEDERAL ADMINISTRATIVE RE-
SEARCH)
State (See STATE ADMINISTRATIVE RE-
SEARCH)

**A.L.R.** (See *AMERICAN LAW REPORTS (A.L.R.)*)

*AMERICAN LAW REPORTS (A.L.R.)*
Generally . . . 2[C][5]
Electronic version . . . 2[C][5][b]
Print version
   Generally . . . 2[C][5][a]; 2[C][5][a][i]
   Annotation, finding and updating
    . . . 2[C][5][a][ii]; 2[C][5][a][iii]
   Case law, updating . . . 2[C][5][a][iv]

**ATTORNEY GENERAL OPINIONS**
Generally . . . 9[B][1]
Description . . . 9[B][1][a]
Location methods
   Generally . . . 9[B][1][d]
   Electronic version . . . 9[B][1][d][ii]
   Internet version . . . 9[B][1][d][iii]
   Print version . . . 9[B][1][d][i]
Purpose . . . 9[B][1][b]
Use . . . 9[B][1][c]

## C

**CASE LAW LOCATION METHODS**
Generally . . . 2[C]
*American Law Reports (A.L.R.)* (See *AMERICAN
LAW REPORTS (A.L.R.)*)
Definitional method
   Generally . . . 2[C][2]
   Electronic version
    Black's law dictionary . . . 2[C][2][c];
      2[C][2][c][ii]
    Digest edition . . . 2[C][2][b]; 2[C][2][b][ii]
    Permanent edition . . . 2[C][2][a];
      2[C][2][a][ii]
   Print version
    Black's law dictionary . . . 2[C][2][c];
      2[C][2][c][i]
    Digest edition . . . 2[C][2][b]; 2[C][2][b][i]
    Permanent edition . . . 2[C][2][a];
      2[C][2][a][i]
Descriptive word method
   Generally . . . 2[C][3]
   Electronic version . . . 2[C][3][b]
   Print version . . . 2[C][3][a]
Name method
   Generally . . . 2[C][1]

**CASE LAW LOCATION METHODS**—Cont.
Name method—Cont.
   Electronic version
    Defendant's name . . . 2[C][1][b];
      2[C][1][b][ii]
    Plaintiff's name . . . 2[C][1][a]; 2[C][1][a][ii]
    Popular name . . . 2[C][1][c]; 2[C][1][c][ii]
   Internet version
    Defendant's name . . . 2[C][1][b];
      2[C][1][b][iii]
    Plaintiff's name . . . 2[C][1][a];
      2[C][1][a][iii]
   Print version
    Defendant's name . . . 2[C][1][b];
      2[C][1][b][i]
    Plaintiff's name . . . 2[C][1][a]; 2[C][1][a][i]
    Popular name . . . 2[C][1][c]; 2[C][1][c][i]
Topic method
   Generally . . . 2[C][4]
   Electronic version . . . 2[C][4][b]
   Print version . . . 2[C][4][a]

**CASE LAW RESEARCH**
Generally . . . 2[A]
Court system . . . 2[A][3]
Foundation . . . 2[A][2]
Legal authority
   Primary authority . . . 2[A][1][a]
   Secondary authority . . . 2[A][1][b]
Location methods (See CASE LAW LOCATION
METHODS)
Organization of case laws
   Generally . . . 2[B]
   *American Law Reports (A.L.R.)* (See *American
Law Reports (A.L.R.)*)
   Official reports . . . 2[B][1]
   Publication stages
    Generally . . . 2[B][3]
    Advance sheets . . . 2[B][3][b]
    Bound volumes . . . 2[B][3][c]
    Slip opinions . . . 2[B][3][a]
   Reported cases
    Generally . . . 2[B][2]
    Geography, based on . . . 2[B][2][b]
    Jurisdiction, based on . . . 2[B][2][a]
    Subject matter, based on . . . 2[B][2][c]
   Subject access . . . 2[B][4]
   Unofficial reports . . . 2[B][1]
Types of authority (See LEGAL AUTHORITY)

**CITATIONS**
Case law legal sources . . . 2[D]
Form . . . 1[F]

**CITIES** (See MUNICIPAL LEGISLATION)

**CONSTITUTIONAL LAW RESEARCH**
Constitutional provision, finding and updating
   Generally . . . 3[C]
   Electronic version . . . 3[C][2]

[References are to sections.]

[References are to sections.]

[References are to sections.]

[References are to sections.]